# RUN
## FOR YOUR LiFE

# RUN
## FOR YOUR LiFE

## Mindful running for a happy life

## WiLLiAM PULLEN

PENGUIN LIFE

UK | USA | Canada | Ireland | Australia
India | New Zealand | South Africa

Penguin Life is part of the Penguin Random House group of companies
whose addresses can be found at global.penguinrandomhouse.com

Penguin
Random House
UK

First published 2017
001

Footprint image © Szikszaizsu/Shutterstock

Set in 11.5/16.75 pt ITC Stone Serif Std
Typeset by Jouve (UK), Milton Keynes
Printed in Great Britain by Clays Ltd, St Ives plc

A CIP catalogue record for this book is available from the British Library

ISBN: 978–0–241–26282–5

# CONTENTS

# ACKNOWLEDGEMENTS

I'd like to thank fellow therapists Joanna Green, Lucy Johnson, Camille De Stempel and Mark Boyden. I'd also like to thank my family and all my teachers along the road.

# INTRODUCTION

## What is Dynamic Running Therapy?

*Movement is medicine*

Have you ever been on a long walk in the fresh air, either alone or with friends, and suddenly had that moment of clarity where all things in life slot into place? Ever gone for a run when your mind is whirring from a busy day in the office and returned home, exhausted, sweaty but with a new take on the events of the past day? At its most fundamental that feeling, that clarity, is the basis of Dynamic Running Therapy, or DRT.

DRT is a powerful and engaging step-by-step therapeutic method for confronting difficult feelings and circumstances in your life through movement. By bringing together exercise, talk therapy and the ancient wisdom of mindfulness, it allows you to return to a healthy, fulfilled life. While mindfulness traditionally focuses on the sensations of the body and the environment to ground you in the present, this practice goes a step further. DRT uses the movement of your body to get you closer to what is going on inside you emotionally, helping you to both understand and process it better. This dynamic method offers a more empowering and proactive route to recovery than traditional therapy, adding a sense of competency and personal achievement to your journey.

DRT can also be adapted to whatever level of fitness you have as long as you are challenging yourself physically some degree some of the time. This means that if a walk is a struggle for you, that counts as DRT. Likewise, if sprinting is your thing then you can set that as your DRT pace. The goal is to find a level of challenge where the blood starts to flow a little faster. There is no need to push yourself too hard or to maintain the same pace throughout the session. Feel free to mix it up, minute by minute, session by session. And for days when the rain or the pain is too much, a session spent sitting inside is just fine.

> *To me, if life boils down to one thing, it's movement.*
> *To live is to keep moving.*
> **JERRY SEINFELD**

Anyone who has found themselves opening up to a friend on a long walk or road trip will be familiar with the sense of ease that comes from talking and moving at the same time. The words seem to flow, tumbling from story to story. Transfixed by the momentum, you find yourself travelling down an unfolding path in your mind. You may not see where it's leading, and yet you feel no urge to stop. On the contrary, though you might not understand the significance of what you're saying, a sense of the importance of the moment grips you. Secrets, seldom shared before, fall into the conversation with surprising ease. When silence comes it seems to be a natural part of the journey, the moving road ahead somehow holding the 'togetherness' of you in place. Some people call this sensation 'flow' – the phenomenon whereby it feels as if you are exactly where you are supposed to be, doing exactly what you are supposed to be doing, at exactly this moment.

DRT doesn't promise that you will experience flow continuously, but because it unites talk therapy with movement it is a practice in which flow often arises. The fact is, movement is healing – a medicine not just for the body but also for the mind and soul. We know this in our bones and in our hearts. Movement is instinctive and written deep into our DNA – it is why we experience the flow described above and why our hips begin to sway at the sound of a beat.

So, why learn from only the spoken word, or thoughts, when the moving body is so informative? The body screams out in communication and can tell you everything, from what makes you happy and sad to what you do with stress and anger. Your slumped posture reflects how heavily the world weighs down on you this wet and windy Monday morning. The spring in your step today could be a consequence of your promotion yesterday. How you run may indicate how you move in the wider world, such as in your relationships or work life. Are you quick to start but tire rapidly? Are you consistently paced but just can't let go? Or perhaps you're all about the sprint finish, forgetting that the detail of how you start the run is important too?

## What DRT Is

- DRT is an open-ended practice, continuing until you decide to stop.
- It is led by you, so is as physically challenging as you choose.
- It is as much about sitting and walking – grounding yourself, and being present in various stages of movement – as it is about running.
- It is proactive – a physical enactment of the feelings in your life and changes that you want.

## What DRT Is Not

- It is not a new kind of exercise regime.
- It is not a get-fit-quick routine – physical, mental, or emotional.
- It is not all about running.
- It does not require a high level of fitness.

Movement is critical in our lives. Often, in order to grow or to overcome strife we need a sense of undergoing a passage or transition. Movement shifts perspective and, in so doing, provides clarity, firing up hope, drive and possibility. Critical to the power of this practice is a phenomenon referred to as 'emotion in motion', the sensation of feeling full of and connected to our feelings as we move. We may begin to connect with feelings that are hidden deep down. As we start to move our emotions rise up, enlivened by the energy we exert and the story we are telling ourselves. It is as though somehow the movement becomes an enactment or performance of our inner emotions. This 'acting out' of what's inside can lead to a greater sense of ownership of who we are, as though we are more aligned with ourselves. This powerful process of walking or running with, into or through our feelings can be amazingly insightful and liberating and is the bedrock of DRT.

Sometimes the experience is about familiarization, about getting closer to and knowing more about the specific emotion. Other times it's painful, more about allowing suppressed emotion to flow freely at last. And then sometimes it is about nothing more than quietly moving forward, engaged with a fuller sense of who we are and our place in the world.

Whether alone or with a friend, be aware of what you are embarking on. It is important to respect the power this process has and to make it your ally. A momentum often develops which can lead to surprising revelations – moments of illumination when suddenly the truth of a particular memory becomes clear or a detail is remembered for the first time. Or it could be you experience the fullness of a feeling in a way you never have before. This can be pleasant or painful. It might be recalling a special moment or compliment whose significance in your life is only now made clear, or perhaps a dreaded confrontation with a loved one or the breakup of an important relationship. Take it slowly, there is no rush. Don't push yourself or feel under pressure to disclose if with a friend.

### Avoid Striving

It is important that maximum care be taken to avoid 'striving' while doing DRT. Striving is the bedfellow of anxiety and a modern curse of the first order. Understanding and healing are best achieved by clearing a path in front of them, not by crashing into and through them. Peace is not found through continuous pushing. There is no use in trying to run as far as possible as fast as possible while understanding as much as possible. As you progress you will find your pace and your footing – don't try to rush to the end.

## The Development of Dynamic Running Therapy

The first footsteps of Dynamic Running Therapy trace a circle along the path that surrounds the Serpentine lake in London's Hyde Park. The park sits in the heart of the metropolis and in the summer of 2007 was to be my home away from home, and a refuge from the noisy city around me and the madness in my mind. Its leafy nooks and crannies, its quiet corners and hidden hillocks became my green asylum. When I was in the park, I felt a sense of space. The thoughts that ordinarily flooded my mind seemed to quieten just a little. Much to my surprise, I also found my vocation there, among the trees and birds.

Like most of us, I have lived a life full of ups and downs. I've made a few poor decisions, some good ones too, and at times a few that others might call extreme. To me they were all just steps on my path – I was doing the best I could with what I had, as we all do. It is important not to allow the narrative of what has happened to us over the years take precedence over our responsibility to address it today. Healing often takes place through the process of recognizing the choices made along the journey rather than by reliving it continuously, and that potential increases when you understand the part you have played in reaching your present position. What I came to learn in Hyde Park that summer was that, just like everyone else, no matter how powerful my avoidance or detachment may have been in the past, I had to accept responsibility for many of my worst decisions. But most importantly I began to see that the real problem wasn't with what had happened to me in the past but rather with how I related to myself in the present. I had to first learn how even to value a relationship with myself, and then how to do it well.

My own journey included many a twist and turn, some bright moments and some awful ones. I knew of the rejuvenating qualities of exercise and fresh air, so for my darkest moments I made this central to my recovery plan. I began to run almost daily around the Serpentine. Being a lifelong smoker meant at first I could barely do quarter of a mile. In time this became half a mile and then a mile. I remember fondly the day I did my first whole lap – two miles. I was rediscovering not just my strength but parts of myself that had been dormant for years. I became energized and filled with a sense of possibility – the very opposite of the depressive thoughts I had felt before. The welcome sight of hope began to appear. It took many a month and many a step, including a few backwards, but in time I found enough movement to get out of my hole.

I was not alone on that hallowed ground. The company I found for my runs during those difficult days was a blessing. My partner was a friend with his own battle raging. He was at the early stages of a relationship breakdown that would end in divorce. Running together brought more than just a life-saving camaraderie: I discovered that it also helped open both of us up. It drew forth what previously had boiled away down deep all day, bringing it to the surface where I could access it. Strangely, discussing what had been my inner turmoil seemed not merely OK but essential, as though I had suddenly become possessed by a desire to share. This came as a big surprise. Where had this man come from who had so much to say about life? Who longed to hear the struggles of another? Who felt so comfortable in the midst of so much intimacy?

I looked forward to these runs during which honesty came so easily, and being able to express myself and be heard felt both liberating and healing. But I also felt empowered – I was the captain of my ship, actively steering a course to wellness. A year later I took the leap from my personal therapy and began training to be a therapist myself, a path that would take six years to travel. The training was intense, providing a comprehensive understanding of the history and workings of the different kinds of psychotherapy available today. The variety of institutions I worked in gave me a valuable insight into how people relate to themselves and to others. I learned the importance of patience, silence and space. I also learned about real connection, real empathy and the importance of clarity.

I feel privileged to be able to watch the re-emergence of happiness and hope on the faces of those with whom I practise DRT. To observe stress and anxiety beginning to make room for calm and contentment is a profound experience. Each person has a different mountain to climb or descend and it is an honour to accompany them on those difficult and important first few steps.

## What is DRT Particularly Good For?

*If you can't fly then run; if you can't run then walk;*
*if you can't walk then crawl; but whatever*
*you do you have to keep moving forward.*
MARTIN LUTHER KING

### Becoming Unstuck

Dynamic Running Therapy can be particularly useful for people who feel 'stuck' or worn down, or who suffer low mood, anxiety, stress or depression. This is because the movement involved in DRT 'embodies' or acts out the process of becoming 'unstuck'. Research shows how effective walking and running can be in easing the symptoms of these conditions. Combine this with how empowering it can be to take charge of your situation physically and proactively, one measurable, doable step at a time, and you have a recipe that can create change.

Many people experience feelings of helplessness when confronted with an overwhelming pain or challenge in their lives. Symptoms often include a build-up of stress, difficulty sleeping, irritability, a sense of being alone – the list is almost endless. DRT can provide a sense of empowerment, motivation and accomplishment with which to counter these symptoms, allowing you the space to address what is happening to you on a deeper level.

### Dealing with Anger

Exercise boosts your energy levels and can lessen the mental fatigue often caused by anger and frustration. It can act as an outlet for exasperation and pent-up rage. Again, when you relieve some of the symptoms, you get a chance to look at the underlying situation and the root cause of these emotions.

### Working Through Relationship Problems

The collaborative and trusting atmosphere this process engenders makes for a safer place to discuss difficult subjects like infidelity and sexual dysfunction. This in turn leads to greater self-awareness and self-confidence. When we find ourselves worried about or affected by the behaviour of loved ones, this process can be a useful way to shine a light on both the situation and our reactions to it, and clarify the options we have available to deal with it.

### Working Towards a Goal

DRT is well suited for those hoping to achieve a particular goal or who require help making a decision, because working through each run or walk step by step generates a powerful sense of progression and agency. For this same reason it is well suited for life transitions such as a divorce or changes at work. For those who are grieving it can serve as a useful way to re-engage with hope and life.

## Mindfulness

*It is remarkable how liberating it is to see that your thoughts are just thoughts, and that they are not 'you' or 'reality' . . . the simple act of recognizing your thoughts as thoughts can free you from the distorted reality they often create and allow for more clear-sightedness and a greater sense of manageability in your life.*

JON KABAT-ZINN

Mindfulness has received an enormous amount of attention in recent years, but it has been around for centuries, originating from the Buddhist tradition. A good degree of its popularity can be attributed to Jon Kabat-Zinn, a Buddhist professor at the University of Massachusetts, who developed 'Mindfulness-based Stress Reduction' – a method used all over the world to address stress.

The key concept of mindfulness is to focus on the immediate present rather than the past or future, and do so in a non-judgemental state. It asks you to attend to what is happening around you and in you right at this moment. This includes all the thoughts, emotions and sensations that you are presently experiencing. Awareness without judgment means being entirely open to what is happening in the moment, but not actively forming an opinion as to whether it is pleasant or unpleasant. Should such an opinion appear, let it pass by. After all, opinions are not facts – they come and go, changing from day to day. As you get better at this and mindfulness becomes habitual, you will discover a quiet, judgement-free place within that you can go to at times of stress, or, indeed, just for some peace.

## The Buddha and the Two Arrows

*The Buddha taught that we are hit by two arrows every time something happens in our lives. The first arrow is the event itself. The second arrow is our reaction to the event and all the stuff we add to it. We can't avoid the first arrow but we can learn to do something about the second. By using mindful awareness we can learn to stay with the first arrow more of the time, in so doing avoiding much of the confusion, frustration and rumination brought by the second arrow.*

Each DRT session begins with a four-stage process referred to as grounding, which draws heavily on mindfulness. A detailed guide to grounding is given on pages 21—5. As part of DRT, the process is shorter than in typical mindfulness meditation, but this does help those of us who find it hard to remain still for a long time to achieve that same mindful state.

Dynamic Running Therapy shares with mindfulness a belief that by acknowledging our feelings and thoughts we can make peace with them. We begin to see that there is a way to be separate from our thoughts, that a thought can come and go. This frees us from overidentifying with our thoughts, which so often leads to feelings of being overwhelmed. It also frees us from the self-defeating strategy of trying to avoid or ignore our thoughts and feelings, which often just results in them becoming more worrying or popping up elsewhere.

> *People genuinely believe that if they worry enough over their unhappiness they will eventually find a solution.*
> MARK WILLIAMS AND DANNY PENMAN,
> *MINDFULNESS: FINDING PEACE IN A FRANTIC WORLD*

Most of us know what it is like to ruminate over something until it grows out of all proportion. Many of us do this on a daily basis, using our minds to try to 'think away' unpleasant feelings. As Williams and Penman say in their book, it is not the mood or feeling that does most of the damage – it's your reaction to it. Often we enter into a well-worn habit of identifying the 'problem' feeling and then scanning our minds for an appropriate solution. This often involves rehashing through all the similar 'problems' until we find a match – most of the time as painful a habit as it is futile. Perhaps you then berate yourself for again failing to sort it. This kind of spiralling behaviour does us no good. DRT helps you to let go and instead be more present and accepting.

## How to Use this Book

The first thing is to determine what you want to address with DRT. You perhaps already have a pretty good idea about this, but if you are not sure, then read through the book and try to identify which chapter is most relevant to you. Some readers may recognize themselves in several chapters. This is fine too – after all, we are complex creatures. Don't be afraid to experiment with every aspect of DRT. For instance if you would like an exercise that helps explore your relationship with yourself, you can find this on page 109, 'Running into You', in the chapter on relationships.

The next step is to decide how you would like to practise DRT: would you prefer to run alone, or work with a partner? If you're not sure, the next two chapters will help you to decide which approach might work best for you. Once you've made this decision, you'll be able to start, beginning with the grounding techniques and then progressing into the exercises themselves. There is space in this book to record and reflect on each run. You will find writing down your thoughts and feelings can be a great way to carry you through the process. Above all, remember to take your time and be patient with yourself on your journey. Good luck!

# THE JOURNEY

*If you can see your path laid out in front of you step by step,
you know it's not your path. Your own path you make with
every step you take. That's why it's your path.*

JOSEPH CAMPBELL

## One Step at a Time

Dynamic Running Therapy is not complicated or particularly challenging – it's more about learning a couple of simple but very powerful techniques and embarking on an exploration of who you are. Like most journeys, the important thing is to keep putting one foot in front of the other. Try to practise being mindful of your journey as you continue to move forward – this means being aware of how you experience yourself as you go along. By being aware of your progression on the journey you allow yourself the opportunity to cultivate a more compassionate, gentle and accepting relationship with yourself. Remember, you are not actively changing anything – merely noticing the tone of your inner dialogue and meeting whatever you find there with acceptance and patience, letting it pass on by naturally.

Often in this busy, overstimulated world of ours, we treat

the relationship we have with ourselves as a secondary concern, an afterthought that can be dealt with at some later
date. Often we tell ourselves that we will find time to slow
down tomorrow, change our diet next week, or work on
our self-respect next month. As a result, our relationships
suffer as we grow less connected with the world and those
around us. When we become aware of who we are we can
better reach out to others and enjoy the world more.

It sounds simple. It is simple. But it takes a little discipline and a little commitment. In her TED talk, the author
Elizabeth Gilbert says of her relationship with her creative
inspiration: 'I am not the pipeline, I am a mule.' She is sharing an understanding that creativity comes from hard work
and determination, not by simply making ourselves available. Forming a relationship with yourself is a creative act
that requires playfulness, experimentation and, perhaps
above all, commitment and hard work. We cannot sit back
and expect the world to present itself at our door each
morning carrying a divine plan for the day. To embrace life
fully and achieve our goals we must take those proactive
steps towards them. Sometimes our experiments will fail,
but that is all part of the learning process – it is important
to fail so that you know you have tried.

Sometimes you will hit a dead-end, be it physically, men-
tally or emotionally, but that's OK; stick with the journey
and you will get to where you need to go. It might not
end where you thought it would, and it might take longer
than you thought it would to get there, but persistence will
pay off.

If until now you have struggled to face your troubles and
insecurities head on, you are not alone. The very nature of
life is that it is a constant stream of change, of victory and

loss, of love and betrayal, of birth and death. DRT will help you to engage with and cherish your struggles and triumphs by giving you the space and time to reacquaint yourself with who you truly are.

This process does not offer peace and everlasting life – it offers a way to learn to be more accepting of who you are inside and of the things that have already happened to you and will happen to you in the future. It helps you to value what is real in the here and now, not the stories that you tell yourself. It helps you to stop thinking about what has happened in the past or what might happen in the future and instead appreciate what is happening now.

Self-acceptance improves with practice – it's something you get good at by doing it over and over again. One client I had lost his business, his wife and his mother in the same year. He experienced this as confirmation that nothing that he touched or loved could last, and he believed that the vulnerability he felt inside as a result was as clear to others as it was to him. In time, through our work together and his commitment, he came to see that constant neglect by this same mother during childhood was the root of his own self-neglect. It was a light-bulb moment that illuminated his own responsibility for self-care.

It takes courage to wake up to ourselves. Not being truly at peace with who you are can lead to a lifetime of anxiety; once you stop deceiving yourself, what you find will be refreshing. If your 'truth' is fantasy, such avoidance will not lead to safety or happiness. You can tell yourself that you are happy in your current relationship or that your 'dream job' you worked for many years to achieve is going well, but if those tales are false you will corrode your sense of well-being from the inside out. The real world in front of you is often actually a much simpler place to inhabit than the one in your jumbled mind.

If you are going to embark on the DRT journey then the best advice I can give you is to immerse yourself in the experience as wholeheartedly as you can. Commit yourself to the path ahead. Get moving and keep moving. If at first the steps are small, just keep making them until you're taking long, confident strides forward. Be a kind and gentle mentor to yourself. If you falter, take time to regroup, but keep going. Imagine you are coaching a good friend or a loved one and treat yourself as you would treat them in your situation. The best coaches are patient, understanding, forgiving and inspiring. Be your own champion, give yourself that prematch pep talk and cheer yourself on from the sidelines.

A good coach also teaches the importance of discipline and learning. DRT asks you to learn from yourself as you go along – to register and record your journey, including your imperfect moments. Learning how to coach yourself well means catching yourself when you fall. Try to see each moment of self-criticism as a chance to grow. Value these moments for what they are – frequent opportunities to get better at being kind to and accepting of yourself. It's not very complicated and becomes second nature quite quickly if practised often. Each time you replace self-recrimination with self-acceptance and stay with your practice is a victory. It becomes a celebration of who you are, warts and all. You will also notice how much easier on you it is – it takes much less effort to notice and let go than it does to analyse and chastise.

DRT really is about the journey and not the destination, so be patient and keep moving. Each step you take is your step. It belongs to you and no one else. It is your relation-ship with each moment that fills a lifetime with meaning, not where the path eventually leads.

Bear in mind the words of the celebrated Buddhist teacher Pema Chödrön, as quoted from the Bodhicitta slogans of Atisha:

> *Don't try to be the fastest.*
> *Abandon any hope of fruition.*
> *Don't expect applause.*

Finally, be prepared to struggle a bit. DRT has a way of bringing to the surface really difficult truths about ourselves – the very same truths that can set us free. Along the way fear and shame may emerge. Often they go hand in hand with the most difficult parts of ourselves, the bits we have spent a lifetime trying to disown. Try not to let either get the better of you. This is no easy task. Acknow-ledge and own them as part of your journey and keep on moving. Fear and shame are a kind of 'stuckness' – a getting bogged down in a particular and narrow idea of ourselves. Be mindful, allow them to leave as easily as they arrived. Remember, you are not your thoughts.

## The Right Footing

Setting off on the right footing is important. Try to leave your expectations about both yourself and DRT at home. Try to come to each session with more of an attitude of dis-covery than planning. This is sometimes called 'beginner's mind' because it frees us from the narrow path of historical thinking and opens up new perspectives on our lives. I have an analogy I like about who we think we are vs. who we are:

> I take you into an ice-cream parlour that sells a hundred different varieties and ask you to list the ones you think you will probably like. Chocolate? Cookies and cream? Vanilla almost for sure. Strawberry? You might get to five, ten, even twenty different types. And yet, almost without question, if you tried some of the others you have dismissed you would find among them some very appealing ice-cream. The point is we are much more diverse as people than we think we are, but it takes an open attitude to discover the rest of ourselves.

If you have some negative ideas about yourself, begin the DRT process looking at yourself with gentle eyes. Some of these ideas will have been put into your head as a child, some through experiences as an adult. But they are seldom as fixed as you think. Be willing to discover, experiment and, most of all, come with an open, beginner's mind.

## The Process

Dynamic Running Therapy involves three simple steps. It begins with grounding – a process of mindfulness based on 'checking in' with yourself and your environment. This makes you present and calm, helping prepare you for the second step. This second step is where you will sit/walk/run with whatever question or goal you choose. Finally, we conclude the practice with a moment of reflection on that session in the form of a note-taking exercise, giving you a chance to reflect on what the session has given you. These notes will be important later. *Note*: you might be surprised what the process churns up but record it truthfully and without editing to see the biggest changes in yourself.

## Step One: Grounding

Begin each session with a four-stage grounding process. Grounding draws on cognitive behavioural therapy (CBT) and mindfulness meditation and is a useful way to relax and get in the mood for DRT. In our often busy lives it can take us a long time to centre ourselves amid all the noise. That's why these four mindful stages are so important to begin our practice, making you present with what you are feeling and where you are.

### 1. The Body Scan
Find somewhere you feel comfortable – this could be at home, sitting on a park bench or on a beach – and find stillness. (Or if you prefer and are comfortable lying down, find a peaceful bit of grass.) The body scan's role is to locate you in your own body in the here and now. All too many of us are adrift in the past or worrying about the future. This scan, from the crown of the head to the end of your toes, is ideal for raising levels of awareness and setting up the session. Unfold crossed legs and arms (although sitting cross-legged is fine), take a couple of big breaths and relax.

Notice how your body feels when you're sitting against the grass or bench. Allow your body to settle more fully into the support of whatever you are sitting on. Notice the points of contact and accompanying sensations. Take a couple more big breaths and again, sensing your body's weight, notice how you move with each breath. Allow yourself to settle fully. Release your shoulders downwards, feeling your head gently rising up. Notice how and where your body moves as you breathe. Remember you are not trying to achieve relaxation or anything else. You are just directing your attention to different parts of your body and being aware of the sensations you find there in as much detail as possible. There is no need to judge them or change them. Just try to stay with the experience as best you can – remember, there is no right way or wrong way to do this. It doesn't matter if the experience is pleasurable or not, or if the sensations are strong or barely discernible, or if we find it hard to stay with the practice or not. All of these are part of the practice but we just *notice* them.

Now, beginning with the top of your head, become aware of your body from top to toe. As you work your way down, try to sense each part individually as you go, noticing whatever sensations you may come across. With a friendly curiosity, become aware of how relaxed that part is, or how warm or cold. What does contact with the firmness beneath you feel like? Can you sense the material of your clothing against your body? Notice your forehead, your nose, your top and bottom lips, your chin, the underside of your chin – every inch of you. In some areas there might be no sensation; that is fine, too. If you notice any tension try breathing into it gently, noting what qualities you find there in as much detail as you can. Do the sensations change as you breathe in and out of this place of tension?

Continue down the neck to the shoulders, chest, arms, forearms, and to the end of each finger. Don't try to change what you find or make a judgement about it. You are just noticing, that is all. Now to the groin, thighs and finally down the legs. Finish at the end of either the big or small toe.

During this process, notice how your thoughts come and go. Acknowledge them and let them drift away . . . The goal is to stay in your body, in the moment. Let thoughts come and go and return once more to the practice and your bodily sensations.

## 2. The Environment Scan

Now turn your attention from your body to the environment you are sitting in. Look around, scanning your surroundings slowly, noticing everything your senses pick up. What can you smell? Is it close by? What can you see right in front of you? What is the furthest thing you can see on the horizon? What is the greenest or brightest thing? What are there the most of? What did you fail to see at first? Listen – what can you hear? How many different sounds can you discern? Which are closer and which further away? Which have the highest pitch and which the lowest? Now touch the bench below you or the grass around you. Is it hard? Soft? Warm? Cold? Does it tickle?

As with the body scan, the goal is just to be present, just to notice. You don't have to notice everything, or notice it perfectly. Whatever you become aware of, simply acknowledge and then move on. Become one with the moving sounds and sensations of yourself in this place.

## 3. The Emotion Scan

Similar to the body and environment scans, just notice what you are feeling emotionally right now. Not this week, not today, not this morning; the question is what are you feeling *right now*? By concentrating on the present moment you learn not to confuse what you *have been* feeling with what you *are* feeling. This might seem obvious, but often a closer examination reveals that a subtle shift we had not been aware of has taken place. Perhaps you have several different feelings simultaneously, which can be confusing – there is no need to identify what they are, just be aware of them. The important thing is not to judge them as pleasant or unpleasant, but to be present.

## 4. Priming

The fourth and final stage of the grounding process offers a moment to reflect on what you want from the session. Choose a question that feels relevant to you from the list in your chosen chapter, or experiment with questions of your own, see what feels right for you today. As you now set off on your walk or run you do so carrying with you your focus on this question. Because you have chosen a focus for the session, as you begin to move you embody or impart a sense of movement into the subject, helping you to explore it. As you progress, your story or your feelings start to flow. Each step feels like it is taking you further into it, giving you a sense of ownership and momentum. This ability to engage with your struggles on a bodily level, to quite literally step into your own life and feelings, is what makes DRT such a powerful tool for growth and change.

If you are planning to run alone, you may even want to state out loud the chosen focus of your run. For instance: 'Where does the majority of my anxiety come from?' Identifying a focus for yourself, together with saying it out loud, can be a powerful action, granting you a sense of owner-ship and purpose.

If nothing comes to mind to run with, you can either just sit there or begin moving – remember, the choice is always yours. Take a moment to examine your instinct. It's OK to do nothing, to know nothing, to just be. Realizing that you don't know what you want to do is also a kind of knowledge. It's your choice to use the time in the session however you like. Try not to surrender to your expectations or those of others and instead choose what you want for yourself.

## Step Two: Moving with Intention

Mindful movement is simple. It means acknowledging without judgement what comes up on your journey. Notice, acknowledge, then carry on. If you decide today is a day you want to run with a question, the process is the same.

Hold on to the question of the day gently. Allow it to wash around you. The question is a suggested beginning to the session. It's a kind of seed for exploration rather than a roadmap. If you find yourself veering off into other subjects or concerns, that is fine. Where it leads you may or may not be important, but what is always important is noticing how you are with yourself. Look upon yourself with gentle eyes. If you are patient in the process and not demanding, self-acceptance will follow. When you notice some negative inner dialogue, acknowledge it, then carry on. In time you will become more familiar with these thoughts and may respond to them with a 'there I go again' attitude. Let them leave on their way.

Try to get past worries about the right and wrong way of doing DRT. You are fallible. It is crucial that you acknowledge this, so each time thoughts that you could be doing better arise, let them go. Give yourself the chance to do it your way – this means honouring who you are and what you can do right now – mistakes and all. There will be moments of pain and moments of boredom. Learn to respect these moments – like your laziness and fear, they are an important part of your journey. Try to accept the fact you will often fail. We are all imperfect creatures – try to accept and honour your own imperfection. So be patient, it is the greatest gift you can bestow upon yourself – be generous with it!

Deal with the questions in any order you like. Work on them as many times as you like. Do two or more in a session if that feels right. If you have questions of your own that seem important, add them to the list. Trust your instinct.

### Step Three: Take Note

Note-taking is a very valuable tool. Also known as 'journaling', note-taking allows you to gain profound insight into yourself. Putting down on paper what came up for you during your session and your reflections about it allows you relief from carrying it all in your head and heart. When you are feeling overwhelmed it can be extremely helpful to know you have somewhere to 'put' those feelings. Your journal can also be a kind of regular companion, something you know you can turn to whenever you need. As you find your voice through your writing, you can find strength just by picking it up. Most importantly, your notes serve as a record of your journey and will later prove critical to the process of completing your DRT.

In this book you will find places to record thoughts and feelings that are important to you. And ones that are not important. If you have something to say, then jot it down, don't run it through a filter to see if it first feels valuable enough. Try not to edit as you write; instead, just let the words flow. Recording your impressions and feelings serves as a kind of blueprint for the kind of caring, interested relationship with yourself that is at the centre of emotional wellness. So, be patient at first. Take all the time you need . . .

Notice how you are with yourself as you go about your writing. Are you demanding, expecting perfection or pushing yourself to get to the end quickly? Or are you gentle and compassionate? Think how you would talk to someone you care for – it might differ greatly from the way you talk to yourself. It might help to set aside a specific time each day or after each session to make your notes. Making a record of your feelings and thoughts can also be very cathartic, particularly if you are going through a tough period. Somehow the process of writing them down helps to unload them from the mind.

Write about whatever comes into your head: your thoughts, the weather, the terrain you covered, the people you passed or ran with, your bodily experience and your changing relationship with each of these. You can do this in this book, in your diary or even on your phone.

As Carl Jung wrote, 'What you resist, persists.' So, rather than resisting them, try validating the doubts and fears in your head instead. Then make a note of them. Become familiar with those thoughts like old friends. Don't worry about the quality of your writing. It may be that your spelling isn't very good; if so, it's better to acknowledge that fact than try to push it away. Reflect on how serious a crime your poor spelling is in the grand scheme of things; perhaps it's not so bad as you thought. Many very intelligent people are terrible spellers. Are your expectations of your-self unrealistic? Put other indictments through the same filter.

Try to keep a record of how acknowledging your experi-ence in this way changes the way your discomfort is perceived. Become familiar with the tone in your head and the attitude with which you think and write. Ask yourself, 'Am I gentle and patient with myself or judgmental and harsh?' Make a note of this process, then ask yourself, 'Does it feel better when I write about it?' The goal is to acknow-ledge and befriend your inner critic. This comes from practice and familiarization.

### Creating Your Own Mantra

As you navigate your way through the DRT process you might want to develop a mantra for yourself. In simple terms, a mantra is a sound or group of words possessing psychological or spiritual power. In Sanskrit it means a thought that protects. While doing DRT, you may find that certain ideas, concepts or phrases start to emerge that have personal resonance. Writing things down could start to clarify things for you, or a really helpful thought or idea might surface that you keep referring back to. Maybe you read something in a book or heard some-thing on the radio that really spoke to you. Remain open to such gifts; they emerge for a reason. As the Sufi mys-tic Rumi said, 'What you seek is seeking you.' If you come across such a mantra, take ownership of it and allow it to assist you in your development. It could be a phrase such as 'I know I've done the best I can', or 'I need to know when it's time to stop'. It will most likely be a sentence or phrase that you can apply time and time again to a repetitive and/or disturbing situation, experience or feeling. If it doesn't come to you unbidden, ask yourself what would be really helpful to hear in this scenario. I've had many different mantras over the years. One of the most valuable was 'Go with the feeling, not the thoughts' – a reminder to allow myself to accept unpleasant feelings rather than trying to think or discuss them away. I found it helped me to accept myself as the person I am rather than who I felt I should be. It can take time to find your mantra, so be patient with yourself.

## Finishing Up

Work your way through whichever questions resonate with you. If necessary, revisit any that still feel unresolved. Take notes. Run with your own questions if some occur to you. All of this will take time. Be patient. There is no rush. Let the experience flow and feel organic – this means allowing for times when not much seems to be happening. When you feel you have probably reached the point where you have explored the questions sufficiently, and may have finished with them, remind yourself why you set off in the first place. Has your objective been achieved? Review your session notes if it feels useful. As you go through them, ask yourself if they trigger any subjects you want to explore further – if so, then run with those subjects or questions next time.

This is an intuitive process. If you feel much better than you did when you began, then you are either finished or close to it. If not, try going through some or all of the process again. You will have a strong sense of when you are done. After all, a raised awareness of what is happening inside you will have been one of the most important aspects of your journey.

## Final Synopsis

Dynamic Running Therapy ends with one final and important ritual, the final synopsis. By returning to your original notes and summarizing the journey you have taken, you will get a sense of the beginning, middle and end of the voyage you have undertaken. Rereading your notes can also be highly revealing.

Notice what feelings are evoked as you reread each entry. What was going on for you at that time and what were you really trying to say? Make a note of what seems important to you. See if you can identify a theme or narrative to your journey. You might even want to write your synopsis in a narrative form – a story about your past and present and what you hope for your future. Be conscious of the way in which you write – are you coming at it full of expectation? What is it you want from this exercise? Think about that for a moment.

This final step of getting it all down on paper helps to mark the end of your passage. How long this process takes doesn't matter, nor does the length of the synopsis. Each one is a subjective and private matter. Some will contain more of the past, some more of the future, others mostly the present. There is no right or wrong way to do the final synopsis. Just begin it and see where it leads. You will know when it has become what it needs to be for you. This may mean revisiting it a few times. The important thing is that it be a synopsis of your experience – which means it should give a concise and general overview of your journey. Whether that be your life journey or your DRT journey is up to you. It might even take the form of a poem. It may include the most important thing you have learned along the way or a secret you have never dared to admit to yourself or others. It may be a tale of redemption or a parable about growth. The journey is yours and yours alone. Honour and cherish it. Be proud of your commitment to the path you have travelled. Write with the same honesty and courage with which you have undertaken your DRT.

## Achieving Flow

*It is when we act freely for the sake of the action itself, rather than for ulterior motives, that we learn to become more than what we are.*

MIHALY CSIKSZENTMIHALYI

The concept of flow was developed by the psychologist Mihaly Csikszentmihalyi. It describes a state of complete absorption within the activity being undertaken. It is a state in which time appears to stop and the rest of the world seems to have vanished. Somehow what you are doing feels second nature and totally fulfilling. In DRT, flow takes place on several levels, each feeding the others, creating a powerful loop.

The first of these is via the exercise itself – running produces endorphins which elevate our mood and thinking. This is often called *runner's high*. If you run with a companion, flow is also activated through the oxytocin loop created by sharing, by giving one's trust and attention to another during DRT. Oxytocin is a powerful feelgood hormone sometimes called the 'love hormone' because of its role in social bonding and sexual reproduction.

Flow is also produced through the ritual of storytelling. This is often magnified when combined with movement. Examples of this are Australian aboriginal 'walkabouts', religious pilgrimages and the popularity of hiking. We run into our stories, our past and the present. Most of us will be familiar with this powerful sensation of timeless momentum.

For many, flow will be the favourite and most powerful part of your practice. You may want to experiment with the process first, becoming accustomed to the sensations it provokes in you. Once you get familiar with it, start to experiment. Speed up a little or slow down. When you find yourself beginning to feel 'carried away', try to lean into the experience. Flow can be profoundly cathartic, leading to breakthrough moments.

You may find your flow on a lengthy walk, or a daydream while lying in the long grass, or a jog that feels like it could last for ever. You may be in silence or full of conversation. Whatever the case, savour these moments as you connect with your inner self and your environment. Be mindful of where you are and what you are doing and never be afraid just to stop and take a moment to soak up the feeling.

The most important aspect about flow and its part in DRT is the way in which it gives you a combined sense of momentum and confidence. At times the struggle to get to know ourselves and find self-acceptance can overwhelm us – flow provides bodily and emotional reassurance that we are on the right track and that we have what it takes to get to where we need to go. So allow yourself to trust in it. Just run with it.

# THE HEALING ENVIRONMENT

*We need the tonic of wildness . . .*
*we can never have enough of nature.*
HENRY DAVID THOREAU, *WALDEN:*

*OR, LIFE IN THE WOODS*

The natural world is our natural home. This may sound obvious, but to many it's a forgotten truth. Increasingly, people live in concrete rooms hooked up to screens, far removed from the natural world and its rhythms. The fallout from this disconnected life is further exacerbated by the superficiality of the digital world that makes up our second life. There is so much drawing us away from the grounding and nourishing world around us. But no matter how cut off we may feel, or how far into our own darkness we fall, the sun always rises with the possibilities of the day ahead.

The innate bond we have with the natural world is always within us, no matter how strong our sense of estrangement. It can be felt again in a moment; all that we must do is step outside. When was the last time you lay down in the grass? Gazed up through a canopy of trees at the vast sky above you? In his 1984 book *Biophilia*, biologist E. O. Wilson puts forward a hypothesis that we have a hereditary urge to

connect with nature. He believes this is the result of bio-
logical evolution, a throwback from a time when those who
communed with nature survived longer than those who
did not. This genetic predisposition to prosper from the
outdoors remains alive within our DNA today and is central to the ethos of DRT.

In your practice, make use of the world outside. Nature
has the power to heal and nurture us. But for this to happen we need to spend time in parks and fields, on beaches
and mountains. Even in the most industrial, built-up city
you can find a pocket where the natural world thrives.
Revel in nature wherever you can find it and soon enough
you will see and feel the benefits to your body and mind as
they become more attuned with your natural habitat.
Glenn Albrecht, Professor of Sustainability at Murdoch
University in Western Australia, coined the term 'eutierria'
to describe the euphoria we feel when the distinction
between ourselves and our environment falls away, and for
a moment we become one with the planet. The Swiss adven-
turer and explorer Sarah Marquis speaks of a moment like
this as she opened her tent one morning in the Gobi
Desert:

> I was the wind, I was the sand, I lost my identity as a human,
> flesh-wise. Past that point you don't distinguish yourself
> from nature. We don't understand nature any more but it is
> where we belong.

Nature has incredible healing powers. Environmental
psychologist Roger Ulrich published a ground-breaking
study which concluded that patients recovering from surgery in rooms that overlooked nature required less pain

medication, suffered fewer complications and were discharged sooner than those in rooms facing brick walls. When it comes to mental and physical health, research reveals again and again how healing Mother Nature can be.

The good news is that all that is needed to restore this natural balance is readily available exposure to the outside. Find a path through a wood, a mountain top, a local park or perhaps even your back garden. The Japanese call the practice of going to the woods to heal *shinrin-yoku*, or forest-bathing. Scientifically proven benefits of *shinrin-yoku* include:

- boosted immune system functioning
- reduced blood pressure
- reduced stress
- improved mood
- increased ability to focus, even in children with ADHD
- accelerated recovery from surgery or illness
- improved sleep patterns
- deeper and clearer intuition
- increased energy level and flow
- increased capacity to communicate with the land and its species.

Find somewhere, anywhere, and breathe. Take a bus to get there if needs be. Better still, walk there. Now notice the world around you – smell it and touch it. Sit down and listen to it. Take a moment to enjoy the simple pleasure of being. And be aware that Mother Nature is busy at work on your mind and body, reducing your heart rate, stress levels and blood pressure. You will enjoy many of the same benefits listed above during the grounding process (page 21) that is included in every run.

## Choosing the Right Terrain

*Nature does not hurry, yet everything is accomplished.*
LAO TZU

Choosing the right landscape for your practice is important. The right choice of terrain can enable your experience to be more powerful and enjoyable. How do you know when it's suitable for you? The answer is that every terrain is different, offering specific kinds of feedback. A steep hill may stop you in your tracks, creating an overwhelming sense of futility. From this you may realize just how depressed you are. On the other hand, you may sprint up it, charged with an anger that comes from deep-seated frustration about a situation you can now appreciate the severity of. Don't be afraid to experiment; find out what works for you.

Take Hyde Park in central London as an example. While mostly flat it contains a warren of varying routes, such that you could choose a different path every day if you liked, matching the terrain and challenge with how you feel. Perhaps today you prefer the perimeter path around the park – a challenging four miles. Or maybe on days like this a circuit around the pretty Serpentine lake provides a comforting ambience.

When you feel weighed down, just getting to the park is a victory – there is no need to make things harder by choosing a hilly route which is going to remind you of the heavy burden you already feel. That said, you might decide that the additional sense of achievement experienced by pushing yourself to the top of the hill can create a sense of progress where little has been felt before.

You may feel you want to match the outside with your inside. This is fine, but the land has much to teach us, frequently much more than we imagine. In fact, we often stand to learn a great deal more from an adverse environment than from one that seems agreeable. Hill country can teach us about how we struggle in the face of adversity. A run along a mountain ridge can help us gain perspective on our story. A run along the coast can put us in touch with the timelessness of life. Running the same path repeatedly may provoke an uncomfortable awareness of how repetitive your life has become and spur you to make a change. Every environment and circumstance has something to teach us.

Be mindful of what you need and what you are feeling. Do you want open space – a sense of freedom and possibility – or do you want to be held within the beauty and serenity of a public park or botanical garden? If you are experiencing loneliness, is a place bustling with tourists and children at play more comforting to you than a barren landscape? Or does the barren landscape provide an opportunity for you to both embrace the solitary nature of your life and to notice how, in fact, we are never really alone, as the land is our home? Only you can know what works for you and what the land is teaching you. But for this to happen you have to be conscious of and register the feelings that the environment generates in you. This is also a perfect way to practise being mindful of where you are and how it feels in the here and now.

The Japanese have a word for the space between things, the interval linking one thing with another. The word is *ma*, and it captures the value of noticing what is around us and between us. In the open outdoors we can feel the scale of the world and our place within it. Try to be aware of the silence between sounds.

It is important to remember that DRT is as gentle and slow moving as you want it to be. You set the pace. If you need to stop, then stop; if you need to let go, then let go; if you are working with a partner, their job is to register these choices and reflect them back to you. Together, such information can make you aware of how you move in the world, what changes you are undergoing, where there is resistance – just about anything. If running alone, make a note for yourself of how the landscape is affecting your experience. Try to record this as accurately as possible without judging or interpreting your feelings. Everything has its place, even the mundane.

## Running with a Partner

*What matters in relationships isn't how you see
each other but whether you see each other.*
ERIC MICHA'EL LEVENTHAL

There is something wonderful about being alone in nature, but running with a partner can be a rewarding and intimate experience. Having someone observe your process allows new perspectives to unfold, enabling you to see yourself through a different lens. You are inviting someone to hear your story, your hopes and fears, and to travel with you on your journey of self-exploration.

## Finding the Right Partner

Finding the right partner is ultimately a personal choice and one in which instinct will play a large role. Remember, this is a warts-and-all process – you are allowing yourself to be vulnerable in front of another person. This can be a really powerful experience. It is important to make mindful and considered choices when choosing a running partner. Listen to your inner voice; allow it to guide you in your choices.

Likeability may seem a strange place to start, but finding someone you like is the first step to finding someone you can trust and relax with. Ask yourself if the person you are considering is someone you feel is or might prove to be trustworthy – after all, this person could end up knowing some very personal information about you. Make an agreement between the two of you about the importance of confidentiality.

If it is someone you do not know well, you may want to have a coffee with them first. It might be someone from the gym, or a work colleague, or a good friend. If you do choose a friend, it is important to be conscious of the ways in which DRT may affect your relationship.

Your ideal partner's age and fitness is a matter of common sense – find someone who is of similar capability to yourself and ideally in good health. For this reason, it's important to be a little impertinent and enquire pointedly into any potential partner's level of fitness. You must also be honest with them about your own ability, and discuss any injuries or weaknesses either of you may have. Check with your partner what they would like to happen in the event that either you or they cannot continue with the day's run.

Finally, you may want to discuss what you expect from,

or fear about, sharing your feelings. After all, emotions are quite natural and your sessions should take place in an environment where you feel you can be you. Most of all, remember you are companions on this journey – your role is not to fix or comfort each other, no matter how much you may want to. One of you is talking, one of you is listening. That is all.

## Setting Up the First Session

You will need to agree with your partner on a location – one that suits the two of you. You may also want to agree beforehand on whether you see the session being a walk or a run. You will need to decide who is going to be the listening partner and who the sharing one. It may be that one of you wants a break from talking for a week or two and would prefer the role of listener. This is the area in which disagreements are most likely to arise, so be honest about your hopes or expectations. Don't accept an arrangement that doesn't feel right to you just because you are trying to be fair or polite.

It may be difficult for you if, part-way through the process, your partner feels they no longer need these sessions or succumbs to injury. Keep that in the back of your head as a possibility. Your partner is a companion on your journey, not your keeper.

It is also advisable to undertake at the outset that the partnership will continue until you both agree to end it. This relationship needs to be based on mutual respect and consideration for the other, and ending it is a really important aspect of the process. Agree a schedule – to run together for a couple of weeks, twice per week, perhaps – and at the end of that time review the experience and discuss whether it has been helpful and for how long it will continue. Or perhaps you'll just decide on another schedule followed by a further review. The important thing is to find agreement with your partner beforehand.

In my experience the first session is usually very productive and acquires a life of its own. By that I mean that the excitement of showing up in running gear to 'take on' whatever is troubling you is both invigorating and nerve-racking, usually leading to a lot of energy and talk. If you are the listener it feels like an honour to be entrusted with someone's intimate truths, and if you are the sharer it can be a great relief to get things off your chest. A surprising amount of camaraderie is often built up during this initial encounter.

## How to be the Listening Partner

Generally, the rule in the listening role is that less is more. By this I mean that, if you are in doubt about whether to say something while in the listening role, veer towards not saying it. If your partner chooses to pause or is moving in silence, use this as an opportunity to practise being present and silent. Be mindful of your own impulse to jump in. Try not to act on an urge to fill the silence. Don't be afraid of not knowing how to react or what to do. Your mere presence can be highly therapeutic for your partner and for you. Remember, you don't need to save them, fix them or anything else, just stay with them. They will know that you are not there to heal them or make them feel better. Your job is simply to accompany them.

There are three core conditions of being the listener in DRT. They are simple – easy to achieve and easy to remember. Your goal is to embody these three conditions when listening to your running partner.

### 1 LISTEN WITHOUT JUDGEMENT

Offer your partner a safe place in which to share. One where they feel free to explore and find acceptance for the parts of themselves that are less than noble or that they find shameful. There is no need to indicate approval or disapproval, surprise or agreement. Just stay present.

### 2 LISTEN WITH EMPATHY

Your role is to truly hear what the other person is saying. This does not mean constructing unsolicited theories of your own about what may be behind your partner's problems or coming up with a good solution to them. It means taking in what you hear and empathizing, without interpretation. Here and there you can reflect back any appropriate sympathy you may feel, but keep it to a minimum unless you are confident it is wanted. The idea is that you are present, not totally silent, but mostly. It is their time to talk – your time will come.

### 3 BE PRESENT

Make yourself as personally present and available to your partner as possible during your time together. This calls for you to relate to them in a way that is genuine, not obscured by personal needs to appear caring, interested, attractive, intelligent or successful. So be true to who you really are and let that be a guide for you.

If your partner breaks down emotionally it is important to know how to react. You should have touched on this eventuality before heading out on your run and decided what to do. Some people prefer to run right through it, others want to stop for a moment. Follow their lead. Your default position is as companion – not healer, not mother or father, not best friend. Anger and sadness are natural; allow this to be a time for your partner to be who they are completely, to let it all out. In my experience the camaraderie of moving together, of sharing in this emotional endeavour, creates a safe haven in which words are not needed. Your partner accepts your quietness because you have taken every step with them, reassuring them of your care.

Have faith in the DRT method. The 'love hormone' oxytocin generated by sharing our stories plays an important role in social bonding, producing a calming sensation and powerful feelings of closeness. Because of this phenomenon, there is no need for you to do anything or be anyone. The process works without your input. Remember, when people are distressed the best thing you can do is just stay with them; do not attempt to supply solutions to their predicament. Just acknowledge the moment with your presence.

The only time you need to speak up is when you first start working with your partner and prompt them during the grounding process. The prompting is optional, but it can be both calming and useful. Guide them through each of the four steps of the grounding process (see pages 21–5). The exact wording you use is up to you – your role is simply to remind them of each step.

## How to be the Sharing Partner

If you are using one of the DRT exercises in this book, then you will want to bring along a question from it to run with.

Alternatively, you may have something else in mind, or perhaps you want to carry on from an earlier session. Sometimes you'll just want to get going and see what comes up. Other times you'll want to run in silence. If nothing comes to mind either just sit there or begin walking or running – the choice is always yours.

You may want go slowly with your practice at first. There is plenty of time. Get a sense of your partner and what you feel comfortable telling them. There are many stories we tell ourselves about what other people think of us or how we appear. Try to put them aside. Here are some things you shouldn't do:

**DON'T TRY TO SOUND INTELLIGENT.** Intelligence has nothing to do with expressing feelings. In fact, it just gets in the way most of the time. Be you, be open. Have faith that people will accept you as you are.

**DON'T TRY TO BE FUNNY.** Comedy is often used as a nervous deflection during uncomfortable moments – better to try to stay with the discomfort than bat it away. That's the whole point of DRT . . .

**DON'T FEEL OBLIGED TO TALK.** Again, speaking unnecessarily is often of way of avoiding genuine expression of feelings. If you have nothing to say, be OK with that. If, on the other hand, you have a lot you need to say, allow it to flow freely.

**DON'T TRY TO GET IT ALL OUT IN ONE SESSION.** A goal which is as unattainable as it is counterproductive. Take your time, breathe. You may well find that the story you think you need to tell is very different from the one that you actually need to tell. Let it reveal itself over time.

**DON'T WORRY ABOUT YOUR PARTNER'S EXPECTATIONS.** This is your session – do what feels right to you. Listen to your body. Listen to your thoughts. Listen to your feelings. Express them any way you need to. Concern yourself with you and you alone.

After a few runs, your partnership should begin to flow. A sense of trust should develop between you. As with any journey the path is often unclear and the destination unknown. There will be times at which you will flounder – that is OK, just try to acknowledge your uncertainty and carry on. There is no right way or wrong way – only your way.

# DEPRESSION AND LOW MOOD

*Freedom is not the absence of commitments, but the ability
to choose – and commit myself to – what is best for me.*
PAULO COELHO, *THE ZAHIR*

'Depression' has become a catch-all expression for a wide range of symptoms, some of which are listed in this chapter. How exactly depression develops remains a mystery. For some it may stem from a chemical imbalance, a traumatic event, giving birth, or substance abuse. For others it may be the result of early childhood wounding, loneliness, diet, or negative patterns of behaviour. Any of these can leave you with a feeling of being powerless or stuck. I've worked with many people who have been afflicted by depression and I'm sure that, even if you haven't suffered a bout of depression yourself, you will know at least one person who has. It is a growing epidemic – the NHS maintains that 10 per cent of the UK population will experience a depressive period at some point in their lives. I suspect the real number is much higher than that.

Depression can manifest itself in many ways. It might be that things haven't felt right to you for as long as you can remember. Perhaps a life-changing event such as redundancy, divorce or bereavement has triggered a decline in your happiness and well-being. In many cases there seems to be no reason for your unhappiness. Depression can strike anyone at any time, no matter what the circumstances.

## Identifying Depression and Low Mood

Depression affects people from all walks of life, including apparently successful people who seem to 'have it all'. There are some signs and symptoms with which you may be familiar that could indicate you are depressed or in a low mood:

Tiredness and loss of energy
Sadness that doesn't go away
Loss of self-confidence and self-esteem
Difficulty concentrating
Not being able to enjoy things that are usually pleasurable
    or interesting
Feeling anxious all the time
Avoiding other people, sometimes even your close friends
Feelings of helplessness and hopelessness
Sleeping problems – difficulties in getting off to sleep
    or waking up much earlier than usual
Very strong feelings of guilt or worthlessness
Finding it hard to function at work/college/school
Loss of appetite
Loss of sex drive and/or other sexual problems
Physical aches and pains
Thinking about suicide and death
Self-harming

If you feel that four or more of these are applicable to you, you may want to ask your doctor if DRT is suitable for you. DRT may not be suitable for you if you have a diagnosis of severe or clinical depression.

## Common Sources of Depression

LIFE EVENTS Major changes in your life can trigger a bout of depression, for example, a redundancy, a relationship breakdown or some kind of abuse.

LOSS Loss comes in many forms such as the loss of someone we love, losing your job or moving house. It might also result from getting old, your children leaving home, or losing part of your personal identity for some other reason.

ANGER Some people refer to depression as frozen anger. For others anger can be a safer emotion to experience than the sadness that lies behind it.

RIGID THINKING When certain thoughts or ways of thinking become rigid or stuck it can lead to inflexibility and depression.

CHILDHOOD EXPERIENCE If you suffered childhood trauma such as abuse or neglect, or you were not taught suitable coping strategies for life's difficulties, it may be particularly hard for you to cope with problems as an adult, which could lead to depression. Shame, guilt and anger are all likely to play their part.

ALCOHOL AND DRUG ABUSE Although such substances may temporarily alleviate your symptoms, they can exaggerate them in the long term and can also signal an underlying problem.

**CRUELTY TO SELF** A cruel and persistent inner critic is a common source of depression. It can undermine every moment, every relationship and every chance for happiness. Often connected to perfectionism, insecurity or overly harsh parenting, it can crush all the good out of us.

**CAUSE UNKNOWN** Not all depression has an obvious source. It sometimes arrives out of nowhere, which can make it harder to experience. Often we look for a reason that will legitimize the pain that we are experiencing. If we can't find one it often compounds the shame and confusion.

## How DRT for Depression/Low Mood Works

Dynamic Running Therapy addresses depression via both mind and body. This two-pronged approach allows you to tackle the feelings of powerlessness and futility that often accompany depression. This gives you an opportunity to do more than just wait for it to pass or talk about it – it gives you a proactive means of working through it.

By showing up and getting moving you are embodying your decision to change. There is extensive research demonstrating the link between exercise and improved mood. According to a 2006 Dutch study of 19,288 twins and their families, those who exercised were 'less anxious, less depressed, less neurotic, and also more socially outgoing'.

On this journey you will start to explore your inner world. By becoming increasingly familiar with your thoughts, feelings, emotions and perceptions you will have a better understanding of how you operate in the world, allowing you to make the changes you can see you want. Through DRT and the questioning process, you will gain a better understanding of your depression, allowing you to see yourself with fresh insight, helping you to change what you can and accept what you can't.

Part of the process is based upon our innate tendency as humans to want to develop and maintain our health. Like plants, we naturally grow towards the light. Another way of looking at this is that we are not trying to acquire something which is lacking; instead we are realizing what is already inside us. It is a positive way of approaching life – if we provide ourselves with the right environment, like a plant we will grow and flourish. This may mean having to look at our life choices and the way we take care of ourselves. Is it time for you to start taking care of yourself? Taking exercise, eating well, setting time aside for oneself, volunteering, joining a class, going for walks or any other life-affirming action can help create an environment in which we can start to heal.

The pain you feel when you are depressed provides an ongoing opportunity to improve your mindful practice. Each time you feel the bark of the black dog it is a chance to come back once more to the body, to sensation, and to recognize that thoughts come and go, feelings come and go. Of course, this is not easy at first. In the beginning, the practice is difficult. It takes time to get hold of it. Like a muscle, it needs flexing. But with practice you will see that there is an option available to you at these times – to acknowledge the thought or feeling as just that, and to let it pass on by.

## Keeping Track: Mood Diaries and Journals

A mood diary can be a very effective way to become familiar with your depression and important details of how and when it affects you. By tracking your moods, you are able to see what events have the worst effects on you, and at what times of day. Often patterns will reveal themselves. You can then learn to adapt to these times and situations, making changes to them when you can and preparing yourself when you can't. Mood diaries can be bought in bookshops, downloaded or even filled in online. Or you can just create your own.

You may want to try journaling. Try to put a regular time aside - for instance, first thing in the morning or last thing at night - and record your feelings and thoughts. There is no need to interpret them if you don't want to. The important thing is to get them down as they occur in you and to you. Try to be faithful to your experience. You will find that putting these things down on paper will provide relief - better out than in. Journaling also provides a sort of welcome companion on your DRT journey.

## Questions About Depression and Low Mood

These questions are specifically designed to help you explore and gain awareness of your process, in so doing reducing the symptoms of your depression or low mood. Choose questions that seem to resonate with you. Allow your intuition to inform your choice. Remember, there are no right or wrong answers. If you have questions of your own, add them to the list in the space provided at the end of the chapter.

What do the words depression/low mood mean to you?

_____

_____

_____

_____

_____

_____

_____

_____

_____

_____

_____

_____

_____

When did these feelings begin? How long have you felt this way – was it a gradual decline or a sudden sense of sadness? Sometimes it's good to look at the process so that we can try and understand where the emotions have come from rather than be engulfed by them.

_____

_____

_____

_____

_____

_____

_____

_____

Is there a history of depression/low mood in your family?

_____

_____

_____

_____

_____

_____

_____

_____

It's often helpful to think about when your depression is worse and when it's better. What makes it better or worse? Are there certain situations that trigger your depression/low mood?

_____

_____

_____

_____

_____

_____

_____

_____

Have you thought about keeping a 'mood-diary'? Do you think it might be a useful way to track and address those times of day when you are most prone to feeling low?

_____

_____

_____

_____

_____

_____

_____

_____

If you had to describe this depressed feeling visually, what would it look like? (*A dark black cloud over my head; a swirling mist; a black dog, a jumble of colours . . .*)

_____

_____

_____

_____

_____

_____

_____

How else would you describe it in terms of your senses? How does it sound, taste, smell and feel? (*Loud; a bitter taste; an acrid smell; shivering; sweating; an ache in the pit of my stomach . . .*)

_____

_____

_____

_____

_____

_____

_____

_____

If you had to give your depression a name to make it unique to you, what would it be? What does this name mean to you? Personifying your depression or mood can help you take a step back, to be more objective and less enmeshed in it.

_____

_____

_____

_____

_____

_____

_____

Does your depression feel like it's your fault? Or someone else's? Or no one's? If you do think it's your fault, do you think your friends and family would agree with you?

_____

_____

_____

_____

_____

_____

_____

_____

How would you like others to treat you while you're feeling like this? If a friend came to you with the same emotions that you are feeling, how would you help them? What would you try to do or say?

_____

_____

_____

_____

_____

_____

What are your expectations of yourself and others with depression and low mood? Do you 'beat yourself up' for having these feelings sometimes? Are you compassionate towards yourself?

_____

_____

_____

_____

_____

_____

_____

_____

Do you sometimes allow this feeling to become an excuse not to participate fully in life? What have you avoided doing and why? Maybe you have an underlying fear of rejection or failure, or some other fear.

_____

_____

_____

_____

_____

_____

_____

_____

Are you striving towards perfectionism? How does it affect you? Where does it come from? How does it serve you? Do you think there are people who feel truly perfect, or that perfection is attainable?

_____

_____

_____

_____

_____

_____

_____

_____

How would you describe the way in which you talk to yourself about your depression/low mood? Would you talk to others this way? If not, how do you understand the difference?

_____

_____

_____

_____

_____

_____

_____

_____

Are some of the thoughts that you have been having repetitive? If so, which ones? Are some rational and some completely irrational? Do you feel confident you can tell the difference? Would it help to make a list of both?

_____

_____

_____

_____

_____

_____

_____

_____

Are you prone to isolating? Why is that and what could you do to feel more connected to people?

_____

_____

_____

_____

_____

_____

_____

_____

_____

Exercise is a powerful way to address depression. Can you think of types of exercise you could do?

_____

_____

_____

_____

_____

_____

_____

_____

_____

Have you considered trying relaxation techniques such as deep breathing, yoga, or meditation?

_____

_____

_____

_____

_____

_____

_____

If your days feel unstructured, have you considered drawing up a healthy routine? A routine, especially if it includes social and healthy activities, can be both reassuring and rewarding.

_____

_____

_____

_____

_____

_____

_____

On the other hand, if you are finding your days are too structured and you feel unable to cope, are there changes, however small, that you could make? Sometimes, it can be the tiniest adjustment that makes a world of difference.

_____

_____

_____

_____

_____

_____

_____

_____

_____

# Your Notes

# Your Notes

# ANXIETY

*What lies behind and what lies before us are tiny matters compared to what lies within us.*

RALPH WALDO EMERSON

## What is Anxiety?

Anxiety is natural to humans, serving us in useful ways such as letting us know when danger is nearby or change needed. It can, however, be problematic when it becomes excessive and uncontrollable, seemingly springing from nowhere and with a detrimental impact on our lives. Your anxiety might be intermittent and mildly irritating, like the kind that nags at you during social occasions such as parties or perhaps when you're feeling lonely. Or it might feel more regular and uncomfortable, a familiar tightness that leaves you feeling on edge and tense most of the time. For some it may be ever-present and overwhelming, the kind that paralyses and exhausts you to the point of despair, leaving you feeling cut off from the world and despondent.

Dynamic Running Therapy can both help you to gain a greater level of comfort with your anxiety and ease the symptoms. Some of those symptoms include:

- restlessness or feeling on edge
- being easily fatigued
- difficulty concentrating or mind going blank
- irritability
- muscle tension
- sleep disturbance
- ruminating on fears and worries.

## Where Does Anxiety Come From?

Your anxiety may be caused by environmental factors (such as social or work situations), medical factors, substance abuse, genetics, brain chemistry, or a combination of these. It is commonly triggered by stress. Stress may come from many sources, including schooling, money worries, work problems, relationship problems, aging, victimization, divorce and grief.

Whatever the source, at one point or another we all experience anxiety to some degree. Unless you are living in a temple and meditating twenty-four hours a day it is unlikely you can avoid it. But, as ever, it is important to concentrate on our relationship with anxiety rather than the thing itself. The psychologist Rollo May understood anxiety in a more positive way, believing it to be mostly unavoidable, natural and the source of all creativity. He saw it as a sensation given off by the struggle that accompanies living, believing that anxiety generates change and growth, pushing us away from stagnancy and isolation. He believed it was at the core of what makes us human and as such a positive force.

How, then, do we experience anxiety in this way? Part of

the answer is to change our relationship with it, recognizing that sometimes it can be as much friend as foe. This may not always be possible. Chronic anxiety can require medical intervention. In most cases, however, unwelcome anxiety can be helped. One such way is to embrace it where possible, rather than try to avoid it. This doesn't mean cherishing every minute you are anxious. Rather, it means learning to acknowledge and tolerate anxiety as the natural accompaniment to much of what we do.

As we evaluate our choices in life, often with unclear outcomes to consider, we experience stress and anxiety. In DRT, the aim is to engage in a positive way with this process of development and experimentation. When you find yourself running with the questions at the end of this chapter, ask yourself how you can harness this anxious energy for good, to create positive change in your life. Maybe you want to ask your boss for a promotion or maybe you want to ask someone out but you are anxious about it, fearing rejection. Try running with those questions in your head or practise asking them out loud, there in the park. Feel the energy the anxiety can offer. Notice how it affects your speed and stamina.

A certain level of anxiety is quite normal. Uncertainty about what to have for lunch or how to pay a debt, about your future, too much choice, decisions about whether to marry or divorce, questions like how and when you will die and, the big one, 'What's it all about?' – each potentially generates anxiety. For some the importance and scale of these 'big ticket' issues lead to unusual or excessive amounts of worry. Others experience a kind of anxiety that seems to come from nowhere, buzzing away in the background for no apparent reason. We live in an age of tremendous freedom, one in which we may choose to follow almost any path. But for some, freedom is an anxiety-provoking struggle. The Danish philosopher Søren Kierkegaard understood this, calling anxiety the 'giddiness of freedom'. We shall now examine various root causes of anxiety to help you explore your own unique relationship with this often troubling aspect of modern life.

## Anxiety from a Past Trauma

For those whose early lives were marked by traumas such as divorce, abuse or bereavement, life can feel scary. If you experienced something like this in your younger years then you may be one of those people who are wary of further exposure to such trauma. Sometimes what follows is a life of avoidance, fearfulness or hyper-sensitivity to entrapment or stress. Often a constant process of evaluation keeps you updated about the specifics of your situation. Am I safe? Where is my next meal coming from? What are my prospects here? Whom can I trust? Do these people like me or will they betray or exploit me? Even though the original drama may have passed long ago, for the body and nervous system it can be like yesterday. Becoming familiar with your 'origin story' can help you make sense of why you still feel anxious. Be gentle, understanding and kind to yourself. Record your journey of discovery in a journal or in this book.

## Anxiety in Your Current Situation

Anxiety may stem from the choices we have made or be the product of our current situation in life. It may be our body's early warning system to remind us that something needs looking at. Often when we try to ignore the need for action the anxiety gets worse until we do something about it. This may be the kind of anxiety we experience when we feel unsatisfied with our lives in some way, or perhaps we are living too fast or too slowly, too safely or too dangerously. Or perhaps we are still seeking closure for something, such as mourning a relationship or someone we love. Maybe we need to make peace with a sibling or friend. Circumstances like these are often felt as a continuous pecking sensation that something is wrong, an inability to relax because something needs to be addressed and, no matter how hard we try to pretend it's OK, our soul knows it really isn't.

The popular social scientist Brené Brown advocates the use of the following technique for addressing 'stuckness' – it goes by the acronym DIG:

**D**eliberate in thought and behaviour

**I**nspired to make new and different choices

**G**oing – as in get going, take action.

If you feel that you are in a rut, make a change. Big or small. Experiment with different kinds of changes. DRT will get you moving on your journey again, helping to point you in the right direction. Note in your journal how it affects your anxiety levels.

## Anxiety from Nowhere

Sometimes anxiety can arise from nowhere, seeming to have no root or cause. When we then examine our lives, searching for its source, and discover nothing, we feel bewildered. And yet it continues. How do we face something we cannot understand? The good news is that not all healing comes through understanding. By experimenting with changes to our lifestyle we can enjoy significant relief from this kind of anxiety. Sometimes it is just about making a change – any change. Similarly to the 'situational' anxiety we just explored, 'anxiety from nowhere' may be all about where you are in your life and what is going on. It may be the result of a lifestyle choice or a relationship/ friendship whose impact you have played down. Try altering some things in your life. It may sound simplistic but it can be surprisingly effective.

As you continue to explore your anxiety using the DRT process you will start to become more familiar with it. Perhaps you will begin to understand anxiety as being an outward expression of your inner world. This in turn may lead to a deeper, more profound understanding of who you really are. You may start to see deeper than you have before, connecting with what is inside you. You may begin to consider what lies beneath your anxiety.

It is sometimes easier for us to experience the anxiety than to examine its cause. It might result from unexpressed anger towards a partner or parent, or a deep loss or regret you haven't addressed. Or could it be a sense of inadequacy? Shame? Fear of failure? Fear of death? It could be that your anxiety has served a purpose, protecting you from something that you are now ready to face. This is challenging work but can lead to profound changes and a reframing of how you think about your life and yourself.

## Likeability Anxiety

Anxiety often stems from an intense desire to be liked, a constant second-guessing as to whether you are deemed good enough in others' eyes. You may have an uncomfortable or troubling sense of this process, leading to a cycle wherein your nervousness creates the very outcome you are anxious to avoid.

DRT breaks the loop in two ways. The first is by getting you into the habit of self-evaluation – not giving the job to others. This simply means training the muscle that routinely projects that evaluation outside yourself to redirect it inwards instead. Replace speculative fear of what may be going on in the heads of others with a concern for how you are treating yourself. Cultivate a kinder inner dialogue.

The second way DRT breaks the 'likeability loop' is through your mindfulness practice. As you get better at this you will develop a growing sense of inner calm. Your mindfulness practice will help you to let go of the ruminating and negative thinking. As a consequence of this, you will find yourself less interested in other people's opinion of you. That repetitive need for reassurance will be replaced by a confidence that inside you is a dependable and benevolent self you can rely on.

## Anxiety from Perfectionism

Many of us continuously strive to perfect ourselves and the world in which we live. This understandable but exhausting goal can be as debilitating as it is futile. While it is natural to organize ourselves within the world with a goal to achieve prosperity, to attempt to rearrange the world around us instead is to court disaster and anxiety. No amount of planning, holding on, controlling or supervision can produce a world that is just as we want it. Worse still, when we are controlling we lose touch with the life that is before us. We end up replacing it with a life we have planned for tomorrow, one in which we will be a different person.

To try to fix yourself is to always begin from a place where you believe you are broken. This is the opposite of the self-acceptance that sits at the heart of DRT. What are your expectations for yourself? Are they realistic? Do you feel you have to do better? Do you bully yourself? How did you learn to do this? Does the voice that castigates you sound familiar? DRT teaches you how to accept and cherish your imperfect self, valuing what you are instead of what you are not. When we let go of the striving, the demands we place upon ourselves and others, we often discover a place of serenity just sitting there waiting for us.

The simple truth is we cannot completely fix ourselves or the world in which we live. Coming to terms with this truth can help alleviate much of the stress and anxiety generated trying to deny it. This may mean developing a mindful approach, finding pleasure in the smallest things, living calmly and gently in the world that is before you, now. This may also include learning to value ourselves just as we are, warts and all. Learning to love your imperfections and the imperfect world in which you live is the first step to being present. Allow yourself to just be you. It is so much easier and more fulfilling than trying to maintain a fantasy.

## Anxiety Due to Loneliness

There is another part of life that is strongly correlated with anxiety and that we tend to undervalue – community. What does this word mean in the age of social media where we have hundreds of friends all over the world? Yet even such a network is insufficient to provide you with the direct contact you need to feel relaxed, valued and connected. Living your life on a computer may, in fact, be a significant generator of anxiety. Your nervous system longs for the satisfaction of real relationships, shared activities and goals. Historically, groups of friends would participate in get-togethers of fireside song and dance. Modern life has long been stripped of many such rituals. Our opportunities for quality time with one another are being encroached upon by ever more prevalent electronica. Ask yourself how tied into your community you are. If you know you want and need more connection, go and get it. Join a choir, a charity, a sports team or a watercolouring course. Just about anything will do. Experiment until you find your thing, your tribe. Alternatively just say hi to your neighbour. Share a beer with them or take over a gift.

## How DRT for Anxiety Works

Dynamic Running Therapy blends mindfulness with talk therapy on the move. This powerful combination is a very effective way to understand and address anxiety. Research has shown that a mindfulness practice is a highly effective tool for reducing anxiety.

Researchers from Johns Hopkins University in the United States examined 19,000 meditation studies, selecting forty-seven well-designed trials that addressed anxiety and stress. Their research concluded that mindfulness meditation can reduce anxiety, depression and pain. Through combining mindfulness with exercise (as mentioned previously, a 2006

Dutch study revealed that those who exercised were 'less anxious, less depressed, less neurotic, and also more socially outgoing'), DRT uses the body as a highly effective tool to manage anxiety.

This approach to anxiety has fourfold benefits. In the first place it directly addresses the sensation via a combination of mindfulness, movement and the outdoors, all of which are proven to reduce anxiety. Secondly, DRT helps you explore your experience, providing a new perspective on your life and your choices. Thirdly, DRT helps you improve your relationship with yourself and your life, allowing for greater self-acceptance. DRT helps you to reach a place where you will discover a kinder, gentler you, helping you to treat yourself with the same care and consideration you reserve for others.

Finally, a rereading and final synopsis of the session notes at the end of the journey provide a sense of completion, reminding you of how far you have come and bestowing a sense of confidence that you now have the tools and self-knowledge to manage your anxiety.

## Questions About Anxiety

The questions here are specifically designed to help you explore and gain awareness of your process, thus reducing the symptoms of your anxiety. Choose questions that seem to resonate with you. Allow your intuition to inform your choice. Remember, there are no right or wrong answers. If you have questions of your own, add them to the list in the space provided at the end of the chapter.

In what ways is the anxiety you feel affecting the quality of your life?

_____

_____

_____

_____

_____

_____

_____

_____

What words would you use to describe the anxiety you feel?

_____

_____

_____

_____

_____

_____

_____

_____

_____

_____

Does your anxiety cause you to feel less confident about yourself at times?

_____

_____

_____

_____

_____

_____

_____

_____

Do you try to avoid or deny certain feelings or facts in your life, and might this contribute to your anxiety?

_____

_____

_____

_____

_____

_____

_____

_____

_____

Does your anxiety stem from a need to address something important in your life?

_____

_____

_____

_____

_____

_____

_____

_____

Have you stopped to think what your life would look like without the extra anxiety you sometimes feel?

_____

_____

_____

_____

_____

_____

_____

_____

Do you place a lot of demands upon yourself and might this contribute to your feelings of anxiety?

_____

_____

_____

_____

_____

_____

_____

_____

_____

Have you explored different approaches to help reduce your anxiety?

_____

_____

_____

_____

_____

_____

_____

_____

_____

If you think about it, do you have any longstanding unhelpful beliefs about yourself?

_____

_____

_____

_____

_____

_____

_____

_____

Do you have a person or people in your life with whom you can share what is really going on?

_____

_____

_____

_____

_____

_____

_____

_____

_____

If you had to write a letter to yourself about your anxiety, what would you write?

_____

_____

_____

_____

_____

_____

_____

_____

_____

Are you prone to black-and-white thinking – the kind that ends up with you feeling things are entirely one way or the other but rarely somewhere in between?

_____

_____

_____

_____

_____

_____

_____

_____

_____

Do you know anyone who suffers from anxiety – how do you feel about their anxiety?

_____

_____

_____

_____

_____

_____

_____

_____

Is there an area of your life in which you feel unfulfilled?

_____

_____

_____

_____

_____

_____

_____

_____

_____

Do you feel that, in your heart, you really want to change your relationship with anxiety?

_____

_____

_____

_____

_____

_____

_____

_____

Are some of your expectations about life and how it should treat you unrealistic?

_____

_____

_____

_____

_____

_____

_____

_____

Are you a perfectionist? This can sometimes lead to anxiety.

_____

_____

_____

_____

_____

_____

_____

_____

_____

Do you believe that some of the anxiety in your life is unavoidable and part of being human?

_____

_____

_____

_____

_____

_____

_____

_____

Often there is a link between overthinking and anxiety. Do you ruminate over things a lot?

_____

_____

_____

_____

_____

_____

_____

_____

If there was one thing, more than any other, that you could do to reduce your excess anxiety, what would it be?

_____

_____

_____

_____

_____

_____

_____

_____

## Your Notes

_____

_____

_____

_____

_____

_____

_____

_____

_____

_____

_____

_____

_____

_____

_____

_____

_____

_____

_____

_____

_____

# Your Notes

# RELATIONSHIPS

*There is a kind of food not taken through the mouth . . .*
*the body and the human personality form a cup.*
*Every time you meet someone, something is poured in.*

RUMI

## What's Going On?

Why, when we each believe ourselves capable of conducting a good and honest relationship, do we so often end up misunderstood and hurt? How can so much pain and anger force their way between two people who clearly care for one another? A good place to start is to consider what we really mean by the term relationship, and what we can realistically expect from one.

The word relationship is used most often in the sense of a connection between two people. Of course, there are many different kinds of connection, each subject to the ebb and flow of life. Sometimes they can be strong and nourishing, at other times weak and wobbly. They may fulfil our wildest dreams or be confusing and anxiety-provoking. In one moment we may feel a great love, only for it to be followed by a tremendous anger a minute later. It's worth pointing out that it would be strange if our relationships were struggle-free. If we remind ourselves of one of the most important elements of all relationships – the entire uniqueness of each and every person – it is easy to see how forgetting this can create a breeding ground for resentment. It has been said that to really love someone is to allow them to be who they are and to grow as they need to, not as we need them to.

## Why Relationships are Hard

Relationships are hard because people are different. It's that simple. There is no reason anyone should agree with anyone about anything. Life is a scary endeavour. For this reason we want our love to be safe, familiar and easy. We expect others to understand and respond to what feel like basic and well-communicated needs.

Many of our problems begin with idealization, starting with the expectation or hope that our sibling, parent, boss or lover will fulfil our long-held fantasies of being truly seen and valued. This is a common source of discontent. After all, in the beginning people generally do their best to please, until finally the veil drops, or the novelty wears off, and the person beneath is revealed.

What often follows is a period of intense self-scrutiny, searching through reams of memories for clues as to how we got into this situation. Mostly this is a fairly defensive enterprise which adds little to its chances of success. Moreover, most pain in relationships comes from a sense of unfulfilled needs, but we often leave it too late to express them and by the time we do so, we do it poorly. The story we tell ourselves is that the other person has been deliberately ignoring our clearly communicated pleas. So in time this leads us to shift the blame onto the other, with a resulting loggerheads situation that many of us will be familiar with.

At the heart of it all is an unspoken list of expectations and assumptions – both of ourselves and of our loved ones. In 1923 the philosopher Martin Buber, writing in his famous book *I and Thou*, spoke of the distinction between an 'I–It' relationship, in which you objectify the other, and an 'I–Thou' relationship, where instead you make an effort to see others as they truly are (while simultaneously allowing your true self to be seen). He believed this led to a more authentic and sacred relationship. He was trying to illustrate the importance of not making lazy assumptions about others or taking them for granted, warning us that when we do this we are only half alive.

## How DRT for Relationships Works

DRT gets you to look at the assumptions, prejudices and expectations that you experience in relationships, and helps to replace them with something more authentic. It does this through an acknowledgement and acceptance of your true self, including the more vulnerable, scared and judgemental parts. This means catching yourself when you fall into any of these traps. In time it gets to be second nature – things like making and sustaining eye contact, being more honest about who you are, asking questions instead of making assumptions, and acknowledging the right of others to be flawed. It means valuing vulnerability, and being open, available and generous.

Accepting the flaws of others begins with accepting your own – relating well with others begins with relating well with yourself. DRT helps you to honour your own individuality, to value yourself just as you are, warts and all. Perhaps you have unrealistic expectations of yourself when in fact, like everyone else, you are a complex and flawed organism travelling through space on a large rock. Take a moment to reflect on this: how much do you truly accept both your flaws and those of others? Do you believe you are as loveable as the next person. Are you worth as much as them? If not, why not? Are your crimes really so bad? This is a great subject to run with.

DRT doesn't claim to have a simple one-size-fits-all solution to relationship problems. But it does offer a clear process for exploring your situation – including patterns of behaviour and the drivers behind them. It does this through providing a list of questions with which to run. In time, as you move and contemplate what these mean to you, and the feelings they produce, you will find it easier to get in touch with, and recognize, the emotional truth of your story.

## Person-centred Relating

The other aspect of DRT that is so helpful for relationships is the person-centred element – the practice of relating to oneself in a kind and loving manner. Person-centred relating comprises three elements – unconditional positive regard, empathy and congruence. Each has something important to offer you on your journey to better relationships. As you read through their descriptions below, ask yourself how often you extend them to yourself and others.

### 1. Unconditional Positive Regard

Unconditional positive regard sounds like something complex and intense – in fact it just means looking at yourself and others in a way that is positive, warm and accepting. This simple way of being helps us to remain in an open and receptive place, where we can share each moment in a way that is allowed to unravel naturally, rather than being preloaded with judgement. Think for a moment of how you treat yourself and others. Are you quick to judge? Are you all too often dismissive or condemning of the parts you don't like in yourself or others? Ask yourself if you can be more open minded and accepting, recognizing that everyone, including you, has a right to their own opinion and their own path.

Looking kindly at ourselves and others in this way can be hard for some. Many of us know we have loveable parts but all too few of us consider that even our ugly parts might be loveable too. Often these parts are kept at arm's length, starved of care and affection. They are the parts that need it most. If you ask someone who isn't good at loving themselves what loving themselves means, they will often have no idea how it's done. In fact, it's done by simply greeting the parts of yourself you like least with the most patience, care and compassion. A simple acknowledgement of their existence is often enough. By accepting all of yourself like this it becomes easier to accept others.

> . . . the curious paradox is that when I
> accept myself as I am, then I change.
>
> **CARL ROGERS**

## 2. Empathy

Empathy is the practice of attempting to understand things from another person's own frame of reference. Carl Rogers, the American psychologist who first developed person-centred therapy, said of it: 'You lay aside your own views and values in order to enter another's world without prejudice.' Learning how to do this may be the single biggest factor in a healthy relationship with yourself and others. Relating in an empathic way means taking the time to discover what is really happening in you and others, not making assumptions, guesses or quick judgements.

For example, rather than beating yourself up for being needy, you could acknowledge the fact that as a child you were never sure when you were next going to see your mother, and this made you clingy and anxious, constantly watching the front door for when she came home. Suddenly this is less about your own lack of resources and failure and more about how you responded in an understandable way to difficult circumstances as a child. With better understanding like this comes greater tolerance and compassion for yourself and others. By putting you in touch with parts of either yourself or others that have been neglected, often a greater sense of completeness and peace is felt.

## 3. Congruence

Congruence is defined in the dictionary as 'agreement or harmony; compatibility'. Finding your own harmony comes from no longer striving to be someone you are not but instead embracing the real you. We are talking about authenticity. Sounds easy, right? Actually, again, it's really just a matter of practice. DRT helps you to pay attention to those moments when you are berating yourself for not being enough or for being too much and helps you just to BE. In order to BE you just need to be mindful about what you are feeling and sensing, acknowledging what you come across. Striving to get somewhere else or be someone else often creates huge amounts of frustration, anger, disappointment and pain. Harmony is found from aligning ourselves with who we are and doing the same for others. Mindfulness exercises are excellent for both reducing stress and creating a sense of acceptance with the world and people in front of us.

## Seeing More Clearly

Dynamic Running Therapy helps you develop self-acceptance, calm and wisdom, and as such is an ideal way to address problems you may be having in your relationships. As each of these qualities strengthens within you, you will experience an immediate dividend in the way you relate to others and how they relate to you. As you better establish clarity about who you are, your history and your choices, you will be able better to understand the behaviour and motivations of others.

But self-acceptance isn't easy to come by – it doesn't arrive in an Amazon box on a sunny Saturday morning. The good news is that getting better at it is very doable – it takes only a little discipline and commitment. We are not talking about climbing Everest here. Just a couple of weeks or a month can make a sizeable difference. DRT provides three ways to help you gain greater self-acceptance – via the running process, by an improvement in how you relate to yourself, and through mindfulness. You can think of these as the doing/feeling/being parts of yourself.

Can DRT help to reduce bickering with your partner and the tension that comes during and after it? Or make arguments about money, sex or housework any less fraught? Can it make it easier to stomach the differences between you and a sibling or your boss at work? The answer is yes, but it takes a little practice.

One of the keys to dealing with relationship difficulties, as with most issues, is to raise your awareness of the problem. Through the process of running with the following questions, you will have the opportunity to reassess the relationships in your life, learning which relationship patterns you follow. Through this you can gain a fresh insight and a new start.

So take a step into who you are and how you manage difficulties, the influence of your upbringing, your past relationships and your role in them. Try to be really honest with yourself in this process – remember, there is no shame in being flawed. Maybe you are prone to blaming others ('She's just so argumentative') or using circumstances as an excuse ('I'm too busy to see him, I'll get round to it eventually'). Everyone does something like this but all too few acknowledge it. Be ready and willing in the privacy of your DRT practice to be straight with yourself. Running with DRT will help the truth to surface, but it is for you to acknowledge it. Try these three exercises and find what works for you and your relationship.

> **EXERCISE 1: EXPLORATION** is designed to help you uncover the causes and patterns of your particular relationship behaviour. Take your time and feel your way around the questions listed, running with any that feel like they may fit you.

**EXERCISE 2: RUNNING INTO YOU** provides questions with which you can examine and acknowledge the quality of your relationship with yourself. It can be very powerful.

**EXERCISE 3: GOING DEEPER** is a safe way for you to discuss and go deeper into what is happening between you and whoever you are struggling with. The exercise works equally well regardless of the type of relationship you share.

### Exercise 1: Exploration

Running with the following questions will help you to evaluate your own style of relating. Some questions pertain more to romantic relationships, some to platonic or familial relationships. Run with the ones that feel appropriate for your situation.

# Questions About Relationships (1)

What kind of relationship do/did your parents have and has it influenced your own?

_____

_____

_____

_____

_____

_____

_____

_____

Do you consider the relationship one has with oneself as important and if so can you describe yours?

_____

_____

_____

_____

_____

_____

_____

_____

Do you have a role you typically play in relationships? For instance, being a 'rock' or a 'pleaser' or a 'rebel'?

_____

_____

_____

_____

_____

_____

_____

_____

What sorts of things do you expect from a relationship? Are some these things unrealistic?

_____

_____

_____

_____

_____

_____

_____

_____

How do you think people experience you in a relationship? As you ask this question of yourself are you conscious of a harsh inner dialogue? If so, can you acknowledge that and try to enquire with more understanding and compassion?

_____

_____

_____

_____

_____

_____

_____

Do you struggle to end relationships even when you know it's time? Do you find it hard to trust people? If so, are you honest with others about this? Is it mostly your responsibility or theirs to fix your trust issues?

_____

_____

_____

_____

_____

_____

_____

_____

Do you find it easy to open up to people you are close to or do you conceal your true feelings? How would you like to be and what would that look like?

_____

_____

_____

_____

_____

_____

_____

_____

_____

Do you often feel let down by people? If so, what's behind that, do you think? Does it feel like it may come from a long-held unmet need?

_____

_____

_____

_____

_____

_____

_____

_____

Are there any patterns in the duration of your relationships? If so, how do you understand this?

_____

_____

_____

_____

_____

_____

_____

_____

Would you say you are somewhat judgemental about people, yourself included? Do you think you have preconceived ideas about various kinds of people and would you do better to loosen them up? If you did, what would this look like? How might it improve all your relationships, including the one with yourself?

_____

_____

_____

_____

_____

_____

_____

_____

Is there a certain type of person you are drawn to? If there is, what are the common traits of these people? What do they offer you?

_____

_____

_____

_____

_____

_____

_____

_____

_____

Do you worry that people won't like you? If so, how does this affect your behaviour?

_____

_____

_____

_____

_____

_____

_____

_____

Are you especially sensitive to criticism? Can you own this or talk to your partner about it?

_____

_____

_____

_____

_____

_____

_____

_____

Is there anger or sadness within you that you are not honest about?

_____

_____

_____

_____

_____

_____

_____

_____

_____

Is there something you find especially hard to tolerate in others? If so, why do you think that is and do you possess something similar in yourself?

_____

_____

_____

_____

_____

_____

_____

What do you do when you're upset with someone? Do you find it hard to confront them? For instance, do you freeze them out? Do you pretend everything is OK but make your disappointment clear in other ways?

_____

_____

_____

_____

_____

_____

_____

Are you honest about your own baggage – what is yours and what belongs to the other person?

_____

_____

_____

_____

_____

_____

_____

_____

_____

What would it take for you to find the courage to open up? What would it look like if you did?

_____

_____

_____

_____

_____

_____

_____

Do you have compassion for your own shortcomings? If not, what gets in the way of your own self-acceptance?

_____

_____

_____

_____

_____

_____

_____

_____

# Your Notes

_____

_____

_____

_____

_____

_____

_____

_____

_____

_____

_____

_____

_____

_____

_____

_____

_____

_____

_____

# Your Notes

## Exercise 2: Running into You

Running with these questions will help you to both explore and familiarize yourself with what goes on inside you at a deeper level. The 'Running into You' exercise brings clarity and a sense of an improved connection with yourself. Some questions call for a good deal of honesty, but try not to shy away from awkward truths – do to them as you have with the other unpleasant feelings we have talked about in this book: acknowledge, accept, move on. Of all the DRT exercises, this one perhaps has the greatest power to create self-acceptance. Remember, whatever comes up, just run with it, then let it go.

## Questions About Relationships (2)

How accepting of yourself are you in general?

_____

_____

_____

_____

_____

_____

_____

_____

What do you find most difficult to accept about yourself and why?

_____

_____

_____

_____

_____

_____

_____

_____

Are you more accepting of others? Why is that, do you think?

_____

_____

_____

_____

_____

_____

_____

_____

_____

What do you struggle most to accept about others?

_____

_____

_____

_____

_____

_____

_____

_____

_____

Would you say you are most likely a better, average or worse person than most?

_____

_____

_____

_____

_____

_____

_____

_____

_____

_____

Is there an aspect of your character you have a lot of shame about? If there is one, what is the big secret about your character that you try to conceal from others?

_____

_____

_____

_____

_____

_____

_____

_____

Does fear play a big part in your life? If so, in what areas?

_____

_____

_____

_____

_____

_____

_____

_____

_____

_____

At what times have you shown most courage in your life?

_____

_____

_____

_____

_____

_____

_____

_____

_____

What do you need most from others?

_____

_____

_____

_____

_____

_____

_____

_____

_____

Have you told others what you need most in your life and, if not, why do you think that is?

_____

_____

_____

_____

_____

_____

_____

_____

_____

What would you have liked more of in your life?

_____

_____

_____

_____

_____

_____

_____

_____

_____

_____

Are you compassionate with yourself – and, if not, why do you think that is?

_____

_____

_____

_____

_____

_____

_____

_____

_____

Do you value gentleness? Do you practise it with yourself? If not, why do you think that is?

_____

_____

_____

_____

_____

_____

_____

_____

_____

Do you have demanding and unrealistic expectations of yourself? If so, can you learn to acknowledge that about yourself so you can let it go just a little?

_____

_____

_____

_____

_____

_____

_____

_____

How did you get those expectations? How did your parents and/or your childhood influence them? What is the most demanding of all the expectations you have of yourself?

_____

_____

_____

_____

_____

_____

_____

Is it realistic to imagine you can reduce those expectations and instead accept who you are?

_____

_____

_____

_____

_____

_____

_____

_____

How do you feel about your level of self-confidence? How would you rate it over the years? What, if anything, has impacted it the most?

_____

_____

_____

_____

_____

_____

_____

_____

Do you have feelings of inadequacy in parts of your life and, if so, what do you do with those feelings?

_____

_____

_____

_____

_____

_____

_____

_____

As a child, what did you learn, or what were you told, about how you should relate to yourself? Were you accused of showing off, or being a 'smart alec'?

_____

_____

_____

_____

_____

_____

_____

Does your relationship with yourself remind you of one of your parents? Can you accept and let go of some of the influence they have had on you?

_____

_____

_____

_____

_____

_____

_____

_____

_____

# Your Notes

# Your Notes

### Exercise 3: Going Deeper

This exercise is specifically designed to help you explore your particular relationship situation – to get deeper into what is really happening. Caution: it can be very powerful and revealing. The combination of the process with running can also be incredibly illuminating and liberating.

**For the Sharing Partner**

1. The grounding exercise (see page 21) is a nice way to calm yourself before entering into what may be a difficult conversation. When finished, run if you feel like it or do the exercise sitting.
2. State your desire to explore this particular topic, asking your partner if now is a good time. Use language that is non-accusatory.
3. Once your partner has confirmed that he or she is ready to listen, begin sharing your experience.
4. Most important: as you begin to discuss the issue, take ownership of the feelings that arise. For instance, say 'When you are late I feel as though . . .' instead of 'When you are late you make me feel . . .'
5. As you describe your experience your partner should only listen. The idea is that you get a chance to really describe what is happening for you in the knowledge that you won't be interrupted and that your partner is really listening.
6. Your partner may prompt you after some silences, asking if there is more about this subject. This is to keep the process going. If you feel comfortable, allow yourself to go deeper.

7. Be patient with yourself as you share, take your time and lower your expectations if needed. There is no right or wrong way to do this.

8. It is OK to be emotional. This is your time, make the most of it, be honest and vulnerable. *Note*: Some displays of emotion may be too much for others and bring the session to an end, so consider the impact of your actions.

9. Allow space for silence during this process. Silence is a form of expression too.

10. When you have said all you want to, thank your partner for listening.

You may experience what Brené Brown calls a 'vulnerability hangover' – a sense of feeling highly exposed and that you have said too much. Allow space for this, it's quite natural. It will pass.

## For the Listening Partner

1. The grounding exercise (see page 21) is a nice way to calm yourself before entering into what may be a difficult conversation.

2. When your partner states their wish to explore this particular subject, confirm that you are ready to listen.

3. Important: it is your job to listen. Don't interrupt, don't volunteer ideas, opinions, your own experience, or anything else that either breaks their flow or brings the focus away from THEIR experience.

4. Listen closely, really try to hear what your partner is saying, observe the pauses, the choice of words, the tone, the body language . . .

5. You'll be amazed how much they have to say and what you will learn about them during this process – few people are given a platform in life where they are really listened to.

6. If you hear something that hurts you or you disagree with, let it pass by. This is your partner's moment to talk. Learning to acknowledge and validate other people's experiences even when they don't fit with our version of them is critical to healthy relating. If they become very emotional, try to remain steady. You are there mostly to listen, not react or fix.

7. Accept periods of silence ... they have a place too. Allow the process and place to hold you both. Enjoy sitting, walking or running quietly. Try to let go a little and just be present to what is happening.

8. If and when it seems appropriate, ask your partner if there is more to their story. Called 'laddering', this process encourages them to go deeper into their experiences, perhaps into very personal and historical places.

9. When your partner tells you they have finished sharing, avoid getting into a post-mortem. Allow yourself time to absorb and reflect on what you have heard. Remember, this is still their moment, don't ruin that by now making it yours.

10. It's always nice to just thank them for having the courage to share.

Be patient, fair and gentle with one another during this process. Stick to the format, it works. It won't all be smooth sailing but there is much to learn from the practice. Allow time to reflect on what you have said or heard. Most of all, take your time to respond. If instead you just react you are missing the opportunity provided and wasting your time. Patience and humility should be your watchwords – this is about learning, not persuading.

# Your Notes

# Your Notes

# ANGER

*You will not be punished for your anger;*
*you will be punished by your anger.*
THE BUDDHA

Anger: five letters that together make a word with the power to poison a life. It is the most pernicious of things, gradually and subtly working its way into every corner of your existence: the lover who withholds affection, the critical boss for whom nothing is good enough, the difficult friend who can never admit to anything, the child who won't apologize. We all deal with anger in our own way: there are those who scream and those who simmer, those who blame and those who hate, those who demand it all and those who don't give a damn.

Of course, we are all angry from time to time, and rightfully so. Life is difficult – over the years all sorts of challenges hit us from unlikely sources. Illness, betrayal, embezzlement – anything can show up and bring out the worst in you, making you behave in ways you thought you never could. Disappointment and disapproval abound and then, just when you think you have found some peace, the neighbours put an extension on their house.

Anger comes in many shapes and sizes. It can be

appropriate and liberating. Sometimes it is informative, telling us that we are undergoing a major shift in our life, perhaps cajoling us to change. But it can also catch us by surprise, leaving us feeling out of control. Finding out what is behind the particular sort of anger you are experiencing is the first step to coming to terms with it.

So how to know when the anger you feel is a problem? It's simple, really. Does it *feel* like a problem? In time most people become aware of the degree to which their anger is a problem – either through the strife it creates or through the intervention of a loved one. Anger can destroy your health, your business and every relationship in your life. If you feel it may be a problem for you, do the exercise here in this chapter. The questions will help you get to know it better and find a way to deal with it. Left untreated, anger can lead to a variety of long-term problems such as depression, anxiety, self-harming, addiction and a breakdown in relationships.

## Common Triggers for Anger

### Vulnerability

Often we choose anger rather than risking the vulnerability that comes from being honest. It can be hard to be vulnerable; to express our fears and weaknesses to others is risky and painful. Often we learn this behaviour in childhood and replicate it in adulthood, hoping someone will see through it and help us communicate in the way we have wanted to for so long. Don't make the mistake of believing your partner, friend or boss understands the subtle nuances of your behaviour. It is often better to be clear and direct. It isn't easy, but with a little practice it's not too difficult to become a better communicator.

## Stress

Sometimes when we feel life is stressful we try to exert more control over it, inadvertently creating more stress and anger for ourselves and our loved ones, rather than less. For instance, we may begin to micro-manage those who work for us or become extra critical of our partners and how they care for us. Learning to surrender control is about letting go of fantasies that we can rule the world and make it safe. Ask yourself why you need it to be so safe, what it is you fear about living in a more spontaneous, dis-ordered world. Life changes from one moment to the next – try to pick your battles and loosen up where pos-sible. Easily said but, again, entirely achievable with practice and commitment.

## Unmet Needs

Those needs may include care, attention, respect, safety, freedom and many others. Consider if your life feels safe, rich and fulfilling. Your anger may be an appropriate response to a life that needs change. Notice how and when you get angry and ask yourself what you think your anger is communicating, then ask yourself if there are issues in your life that demand to be addressed.

## Past Trauma

If a wound inside you seems to be the common trigger for your anger, try to get to know it better. Try to meet it with patience and understanding. Often there is an angry child within us, throwing our toys out of the pram when ancient scars are picked at. Whatever the source, show it some care and some consideration. Finally, find some compassion for the wounded self inside you – when you can do this you will be able to do the same for others. Tolerating your own pain will also make it easier to tolerate the pain others cause you. Remember, life is painful, so it is best to develop a useful approach to aggravation.

## Addiction

It may be that you need to take a close look at your lifestyle. Most of us have an addiction of one sort or another. Is yours causing you or your loved ones pain? If the answer is yes, and on some level you know this, then anger is a typical response – especially if others demand changes of you that you are reluctant to make. Addiction can adopt many guises, including online shopping, social media and pornography as well as the more traditional vices such as substance abuse and smoking.

## Disappointment

Maybe someone close betrays you, maybe your coffee comes late. Big or small, disappointment in life is unavoidable. For this reason, it is well worth examining your relationship with disappointment in general. If every time you experience disappointment it provokes serious anger, it may be that you need to look at yourself more closely. With practice, you can learn to distinguish the kind of everyday disappointments that are unavoidable, such as late trains or bad service, from the kind that is rarer and more challenging to deal with, such as infidelity and bereavement.

## Health Problems

Ill health can be a drain on your energy and your ability to focus, leading to further stress and anger. Are you taking care of yourself? Buried anger is often experienced as anxiety. Do you feel anxious? Or perhaps you are depressed – this is often called 'frozen anger'. It may be that you need to reach out for help. Is asking for help something you are allowed to do?

Anger can be treated. There is a way to be calmer and to feel more at peace in the world. Begin by developing tools and activities to keep relaxed – distance yourself from triggers, do exercise, take up yoga or meditation; do whatever it takes to get to a calmer place where you can do some work on yourself. DRT provides a way for you to burn off some of that anger and to look at where it comes from. By creating a closer relationship with yourself, DRT helps you to accept what might have felt unacceptable before – whether that be parts of you or parts of others.

## Mindfulness for Anger

Acknowledgement is the foundation of the peace that sits at the centre of mindful living. This means acknowledging what is happening in this very moment, here and now. If your anger has to do with something in the past then acknowledge that and let it pass, don't try to fight it – this just keeps it alive. Your anger can tell you something about your level of compassion and self-acceptance. Learn from it. Each time it comes to you is an opportunity to practise your mindfulness. Notice how and where it hurts.

If your anger feels like it belongs to what is happening today you should still acknowledge it, then let it go. This is hard to do, but with practice it gets easier. It's another emotion, another thought; it comes, it goes. Observe the coming and going of your emotions without judgement – in time you will become accustomed to the sense of perspective you gain from this. In this way you learn to recognize your anger without the need to act on it.

## How Much Anger is OK?

This is a question only you and those in your life can answer. One understanding of a well-lived life is a life that allows for, and embraces, a full range of emotions – joy, despair, anger, pretty much anything. If you are comfortable with your anger, but perhaps your partner is not, you can explain to them your thinking behind how you express your emotions. It may be an opportunity to get closer to them or even unlock some of their own feelings.

Ultimately, if your friends, colleagues, family or partner finds your anger too much, this then leaves you with a choice: to remain as you are or to find a way to make some changes. DRT offers you a means of getting in touch with your anger, so that you may know it better and channel it out of you. It might even help you redirect it into a positive quality in your life – a useful source of awareness, compassion and energy. Running with your anger allows you to both burn it off and get to know it better. As you examine the questions below notice how your speed changes – ask yourself what this means to you. With my clients I have noticed that when it rises up in them as we run, their pace suddenly increases, sometimes into a full sprint. Watch out for sensations of freedom and surrender – these are important and need to be fully acknowledged so that you recognize your power to intervene and address your anger.

Recent research has confirmed the link between exercise and a reduction in anger. Nathaniel Thom, a stress physiologist, says 'exercise, even a single bout of it, can have a robust prophylactic effect' against the build-up of anger. Thom adds: 'If you know that you're going to be entering into a situation that is likely to make you angry, go for a run first.' Alongside the calming effects of the run itself, DRT offers grounding techniques which will help you to alter your responses in a more constructive way, thereby empowering you to take control of your behaviour and express your anger more appropriately.

At the end of each DRT session, make a note of your

experience. You may want to use this place to keep a diary of your anger, including the triggers, circumstances, timing and severity. This helps you to get to know your type of anger better. Familiarity helps to achieve change. When you can see what is happening for you, you are better placed to adapt your behaviour and circumstances.

## What to Expect

Running with anger is one of the most powerful DRT exercises you can do. It can lead to unexpected places and results. If you are running with a partner it is important they understand that you want the freedom to express yourself in whatever way the run provokes. Be sure they are OK with this before you start so you don't find yourself containing your experience for them. It can be helpful to tell your partner if you think the day's run is going to be particularly emotional for you. Just let them know so they can feel more prepared.

For some, running with anger means raised voices, for others swearing and screaming, others tears, some sobbing, and for some a quiet reckoning as they run into something hidden deep inside themselves. It may also mean erratic speeds and distances as the anger pushes you forward one minute and crushes you the next. Whatever your experience, travel with courage. It is an uncertain path and though it may lead you to uncomfortable places it can be a transformative experience.

Remember, you are in control at all times, so stop if it feels too much. Or go on right into it. Either way make observing the interaction between body and feelings part of your practice. Note how your anger informs your fatigue and speed. In this way, use your body to learn about your anger. There is no way of 'doing it right'. There will be good days and bad but it calls for a level of commitment.

Brené Brown quotes a saying from the Asaro tribe of Papua New Guinea: 'Knowledge is only a rumour until it lives in the muscle.' Running into your anger will help illuminate what is behind it, but you need to put in the miles. You may find that behind your anger lies a great sadness. This may lead to an unexpected deluge of tears. DRT pulls up the truth from your soul. Let the tears fall, it could be their time. Feel free to cry and keep on doing so until you feel you don't want to cry any more. Trust the process and your ability to navigate it.

## How DRT for Anger Works

DRT's approach to anger is fourfold:

1. Through immersing you in mindfulness, movement and the outdoors. Each of these is proven to reduce stress and anger.
2. Through exploring your experience of anger, helping you to identify triggers and aggravators.
3. Through improving your relationship with yourself, raising your awareness of your habits and the tone of your inner dialogue, leading to an improved connection with yourself and a greater self-acceptance.
4. DRT provides a sense of completion – acknowledging the hard work and courage you committed to your

journey. It does this by asking you to go through all your session notes and write a synopsis of the path you have been on, going back as far in your life as seems appropriate. This process helps you find peace with where you have been, acknowledge where you are, and decide how you want your future to be.

### Questions About Anger

The questions here are designed specifically to help you explore your process, gain awareness, and reduce the symptoms of your anger. Choose questions that seem to resonate with you. Allow your intuition to inform your choice. Remember there are no right or wrong answers. If you have questions of your own you can work with one of those instead. Add them to the list in the space provided at the end of the chapter. Begin with the four-step grounding process detailed on pages 21–5 and then proceed with your chosen question on your walk or run.

If some of these questions provoke feelings of anger or inadequacy, or appear judgmental, work with that, but do so slowly. This is an opportunity for you to get close to some painful truths about your needs and your behaviour. Take your time, be gentle with yourself. Practise vulnerability with yourself as a step to practising it with others. Begin by admitting to yourself what may be hard to accept. Meet it with compassion – this is the best way to address anger. Accept your imperfections, don't fight them.

In your childhood, or in your life now, was or is there an unfulfilled core need? If so, can you identify it? Have you communicated this need to your friends, family and/or partner in a useful way?

_____

_____

_____

_____

_____

_____

_____

_____

Have you experienced someone taking advantage of you or an injustice you can't get over? Are you holding on to this pain? If so, what do you get from holding on to it?

_____

_____

_____

_____

_____

_____

_____

_____

How often do you feel your anger is a problem? If so, is it hard to admit that?

_____

_____

_____

_____

_____

_____

_____

_____

What are the major triggers for your anger? Perhaps there are issues in your life around money, work, social or family life, or time. Make a list.

_____

_____

_____

_____

_____

_____

_____

_____

_____

Do you find yourself in a cycle of anger followed by asking for forgiveness?

_____

_____

_____

_____

_____

_____

_____

_____

Where in your body do you feel anger the most? Does it travel through you? If so, draw a picture with arrows showing the path and colour coded for the depth of anger. If it has a shape or character, what would it look like?

_____

_____

_____

_____

_____

_____

_____

_____

Do/did you have controlling, critical or angry parents? If so, how has that affected you?

_____

_____

_____

_____

_____

_____

_____

_____

Have you experienced a childhood trauma such as bereavement, divorce, violence or abuse? If so, do you feel you understand the impact this has had on you?

_____

_____

_____

_____

_____

_____

_____

_____

_____

Do you feel trapped? If so, in what way? Would it help to acknowledge this?

_____

_____

_____

_____

_____

_____

_____

_____

_____

Do you feel powerless? If so, in what way? Would it help to acknowledge this?

_____

_____

_____

_____

_____

_____

_____

_____

_____

Do you feel unnoticed and undervalued? If so, in what way?

_____

_____

_____

_____

_____

_____

_____

_____

_____

Do you own your anger or blame others for it? Try to exchange 'You make me feel ...' with 'I feel ...', thereby owning your feelings.

_____

_____

_____

_____

_____

_____

_____

_____

_____

Do you feel heard? Respected? Understood? What can you do to improve this?

_____

_____

_____

_____

_____

_____

_____

_____

_____

Have you discussed your anger with your partner and/or your family, or are you keeping it to yourself mostly? Do you feel like you can talk about it to people? If not, why not?

_____

_____

_____

_____

_____

_____

_____

_____

Have you asked your friends and family for help or suggestions to deal with your anger?

_____

_____

_____

_____

_____

_____

_____

_____

Are you caught in a cycle of aggression and withdrawal, of push and pull?

_____

_____

_____

_____

_____

_____

_____

_____

_____

How do others respond to your anger? Is it your intention that they should respond in this way?

_____

_____

_____

_____

_____

_____

_____

_____

Can you accept that getting angry is a personal choice and therefore optional? Can you take ultimate responsibility for responding with anger?

_____

_____

_____

_____

_____

_____

_____

_____

What alternative responses to anger triggers can you think
of that might work for you?

_____

_____

_____

_____

_____

_____

_____

_____

Can you distinguish constructive/appropriate anger from
inappropriate anger?

_____

_____

_____

_____

_____

_____

_____

_____

# Your Notes

# Your Notes

# DECISION MAKING

*We all make choices, but in the end our choices make us.*

KEN LEVINE

In very simple terms, a decision is when we make a choice between two or more possible courses of action. That part is common knowledge, but what can be harder to understand are the forces at play when the process becomes complicated and protracted. In everyday life we are constantly making decisions without much thought; whether to have a second helping of pudding, whether to watch *EastEnders* or *Coronation Street*, whether to walk or take the bus. Decisions tend to be based on our intuition (an inherent 'gut feeling' about something with no clear logic) or our reason (based on facts and less emotion-driven), or sometimes a combination of both.

This chapter will be addressing the issues which arise around two most common aspects of decision making:

- When even the smallest decision making becomes problematic and overwhelming.
- When you are struggling with a big decision which could have far-reaching effects and you are stuck.

How we make decisions is a very personal process, informed by things such as our values, needs and upbringing. Most decisions, large or small, don't come from the brilliant processing of reams of data but instead boil down to a simple choice. Describing his experience in a concentration camp, Austrian neurologist and psychiatrist Viktor Frankl wrote: 'Everything can be taken from a man but one thing: the last of the human freedoms – to choose one's attitude in any given set of circumstances, to choose one's own way.' Learning to value your right to make a choice, right or wrong, is an important step along the path to better decision making.

Choice is ultimately how we understand ourselves and the world we live in. Part of this involves deciding what kind of person we want to be and how we want to be seen by others. In this sense it is perhaps the most creative aspect of our lives, a constant defining of who we are and who we want to be. For this reason, decision making can stir up a lot of emotion and energy. It can be empowering, sobering or terrifying. It is important to recognize that these are appropriate responses to such a responsibility.

Part of your journey is to notice the tone and content of your inner dialogue during decision making. Do you play the same record of self-recrimination each time? For instance, each time you consider leaving your unsatisfying job, do you think, 'I hate this job . . . but where else can I go? . . . What if it's worse there? . . . I've screwed things up here, so I probably will there too . . . At least people are used to me here . . . I should have switched careers four years ago when I had a chance . . . I was too scared . . . The truth is I'm a coward . . . I'd better just stay here.' On and on it goes. Each time the same thoughts, the same order, the same conclusion, the same feeling of powerlessness. Although it is hard to see, you are as much stuck in the way you relate to yourself as you are stuck in the job. Change this part and a whole world becomes possible.

Try to listen objectively to this repeating record – better still, make a note of it. Make a drawing so you can see the chain of thoughts in front of you. Look and see if you can identify places in the chain where you can catch yourself – we call these exits. Often you will find that these points are connected to pain and past trauma. Acknowledging that pain makes it easier to let go of it and break the sequence. Sometimes they are linked to fears that have no substance today. This process takes practice but in time it will become second nature. You might want to adopt a mantra (see page 28), one that specifically fits with and addresses your particular chain – a thought that lets you escape its tiring and circular nature.

## General Problems with Making Decisions

When all decisions are problematic, from small to large, it can often be a symptom of another underlying problem such as low self-esteem, depression or feeling stuck in your life. This can come from a lost confidence in your ability or right to make a decision. Maybe not making choices is indicative of a fear of moving forward, or perhaps it is about not wanting to let go of someone or something.

You cannot choose not to choose; making no decision is still a decision. There are many ways we can delude ourselves that we are not up to making choices. For example, not making a choice because you need a guarantee that if you choose X, then Y will happen – this mindset is sabotaging because all choices involve an element of risk. So let's say you want to be sure that if you marry the person you are thinking about marrying, they will always be there for you. Such a guarantee is impossible, right? So what happens? Knowing you cannot resolve the dilemma, you procrastinate and become trapped by fear, and by so doing you extend the problem. Rather than confronting difficult questions about your own insecurities regarding care and abandonment you opt out of the responsibility by loading the decision with an impossible condition.

Some people's experience is more the 'this choice will define who I am' mindset – where everyday decisions feel as though they have an overblown importance, defining who you are and what you stand for. 'If I buy this car, will it look like I'm trying to impress people?' or 'Would this shirt make me appear serious and dull?' By letting you practise regular decision making, starting with the small stuff, DRT can help loosen up such rigid ways of thinking, easing the way into a simpler and more instinctive way of living.

Then there is the 'I just don't know' mindset. This often has to do with your own sense of self – feeling that you just aren't able to make a decision because you honestly don't know what is best for you. This can be a particularly uncomfortable experience. Getting better at this involves a real commitment to getting to know yourself better and learning to listen to what is going on inside you. Because DRT involves running 'into' or 'with' your decision and yourself it is the perfect way to explore who you are and register what is important.

On the other hand, perhaps there is something chaotic

about the way you are making decisions which you then later regret. It is normal to get it wrong sometimes; we learn from our mistakes. However, if it feels that you are continually living off your impulses and allowing passing fancies to take hold, then maybe you are ignoring a deeper unhappiness or dissatisfaction.

Decision making can be thought of as a muscle that needs toning. Practise making decisions on a scale of importance. At the bottom place those daily decisions that don't really matter and practise making them quickly, based on whatever does or doesn't come to mind. Flex your decision-making muscle and in time you will work your way up the list naturally. As you do so your confidence as a decision maker will grow.

## How DRT for Decision Making Works

Dynamic Running Therapy can help you become a better decision maker. You will get to know better and trust more both your instincts and your decision-making process. DRT will help you understand how you relate to yourself and improve your ability to acknowledge your thoughts and feelings. It does this partly through the union of mindfulness and running. Mindfulness helps clear the noise in your head and brings you closer to the subtle and important truths within you. Running helps bring those same instincts up to the surface, allowing you to know physically what feels right.

At its best, decision making comes easily and works out well. However, this cannot be so all the time. Due either to who you are at this point in your life or to the circumstances you find yourself in, decision making can sometimes be a messy affair, full of strife, terror and error. By bringing you closer to yourself in a more compassionate way, DRT helps you to tolerate and care for the less sure parts within you. This in turn puts less pressure on you and your decision-making process. By acknowledging your imperfection and the impossibility of living an error-free life, you can achieve a greater sense of self-acceptance.

The grounding you undertake at the beginning of this process (pages 21–5) will help you experience a further improvement to your decision-making skills. Natalia Karelaia, INSEAD Assistant Professor of Decision Sciences, believes, 'While it's generally accepted that mindfulness helps decision-makers to reach conclusions, there's growing evidence the positive influence goes much further, impacting the way decisions are identified, made, implemented and assessed.'

Mindfulness meditation will give you an added understanding of your priorities and values, in so doing making it easier to feel what is genuinely important to you. It will also allow you space and time to reflect, giving you a sense of connection to your objectives. This won't happen overnight – you will need time to develop your mindfulness practice, but if you can spare just a few minutes a day you should quickly experience an improvement. You will find yourself feeling more authentic, calm and connected with yourself. It's a wonderful way to be in your life.

Mindfulness can make the whole process of decision making less traumatic. Karelaia adds: 'Independent research taken as part of our study found people who are more mindful have a greater tolerance of uncertainty and are more decisive when faced with making a choice despite many unknowns.' By focusing your thoughts on the present instead of the past, mindfulness meditation helps you to concentrate on what needs to be done now rather than recent concerns. By becoming present to yourself in the here and now and not dwelling on the past, you will find unexpected stores of energy and freedom. Finally, studies show that mindful people are less likely to suffer an 'intention–behaviour gap' – the gap between what you intend to do and what you actually do. In other words, practising mindfulness meditation makes you more likely to execute your decision having made it.

## Exercise: Clarity Through Running

This exercise provides you with a way to explore the decision you are considering but does so by also involving your body and movement. Through adding the body, you gain an extra source of feedback. A process of observing how you feel as you move helps you get in touch with your mind and body, leading to greater all-round clarity.

### Step 1
Begin with the grounding process on page 21. This takes only five or ten minutes and will help you to relax and get present to the moment more quickly.

### Step 2
Pause to frame in your mind the decision you need to make, then scan the questions at the end of this chapter, allowing your instincts to pull you in the direction of what feels helpful. If you want to run without a question and just see what comes up, that can work too. Don't push yourself too hard, high expectations won't help – trust the process.

**Step 3**

As you run, notice how your relationship to the decision at hand changes. Keep coming back to the question you chose in Step 2, running with it until you are immersed in it. The further you go, the more likely you are to find clarity – the path ahead will reveal unexpected ways of understanding and relating to your decision. As your hormones kick in, what happens to your thinking?

**Step 4**

Allow yourself to imagine different outcomes to your decision as you run, looking to see how each sits in your body. See what you can learn from your body about decision A versus decision B.

**Step 5**

Try changing the speed and distance you run, while noticing what effect this has on your thinking and feeling. If you are stuck in a rut you may want to push yourself a little harder or try a different question. But remember, you can't force the process.

**Step 6**

Make a note of your thoughts about your decision after you have run – compare these with the thoughts you have noted beforehand. Have your considerations changed? You will be surprised how exercise and the sense of empowerment that comes with it can alter your perspective. Running with the issue gives you a sense of being proactive – no longer just thinking about it, going round and round in circles, but physically doing something about it.

## Step 7

Repeat steps 1–6 until you feel you have come to a decision. You might want to look through all your session notes and write a brief synopsis below of the decision-making journey you have been on. This can help solidify your choice, leaving you with a greater sense of ownership.

# Clarity Through Running: Your Own Experience

_____

_____

_____

_____

_____

_____

_____

_____

_____

_____

_____

_____

_____

_____

_____

_____

_____

_____

_____

## Questions About Decision Making

The questions here are designed specifically to help you explore your process, gain awareness, and allow you to approach decision making with a fresh, more confident outlook. Choose questions that seem to resonate with you. Allow your intuition to inform your choice. Remember there are no right or wrong answers. If you have questions of your own you can work with one of those instead. Add them to the list in the space provided at the end of the chapter. Begin with the four-step grounding process detailed on pages 21–5 and then proceed with your chosen question on your walk or run.

### For Inability to Make Even Day-to-Day Decisions

How do you feel physically when faced with a decision?

_____

_____

_____

_____

_____

_____

_____

_____

_____

What does it mean to you to be a decision maker? Does the thought overwhelm you?

_____

_____

_____

_____

_____

_____

_____

_____

Think of someone you know who is decisive. How do you view them? Do you share any of those traits?

_____

_____

_____

_____

_____

_____

_____

_____

Think of someone you know who is indecisive. How do you view them? Do you share any of those traits?

_____

_____

_____

_____

_____

_____

_____

_____

_____

Would you prefer someone else to make the decision? Does it suit your purposes to present yourself as indecisive? Are you better off without the responsibility?

_____

_____

_____

_____

_____

_____

_____

Is your indecisiveness a new issue or have you always been like this? If it's something new, what may have contributed to the change? Can you identify any triggers? (Does it tie in with a psychological issue, such as depression or low self-esteem, or a certain event, such as redundancy or bereavement?)

_____

_____

_____

_____

_____

_____

_____

_____

Has a lack of self-confidence affected your life? If so, how? Has anything you have done helped to address it?

_____

_____

_____

_____

_____

_____

_____

_____

If this is a historical issue (i.e. you have always felt like this), who made the decisions when you were a child? What are the implications of this?

_____

_____

_____

_____

_____

_____

_____

## For Big Life Decisions

What is your gut feeling about this decision you have to make? Do you allow yourself to include your instinct in the decision-making process?

_____

_____

_____

_____

_____

_____

_____

What do you stand to lose if you make a decision about this?

_____

_____

_____

_____

_____

_____

_____

_____

What do you stand to gain if you make a decision about this?

_____

_____

_____

_____

_____

_____

_____

_____

_____

Can you afford to sit with this dilemma for a while? Is it the right time to be making this decision? What happens if you make no decision?

_____

_____

_____

_____

_____

_____

_____

_____

Would it be helpful to begin a momentum of just making really small and mostly inconsequential decisions and making them quickly so you build up your confidence?

_____

_____

_____

_____

_____

_____

_____

_____

_____

Can you afford to make this decision in terms of finance, time, energy, commitment and/or emotions? If not, what are your options?

_____

_____

_____

_____

_____

_____

_____

## General Exploratory Questions

Do you have a 'record' that keeps playing in your head when you try to make decisions? What does it sound like? Write a transcript for this record and see if you can identify an 'exit' – a place where you can stop it from going around.

_____

_____

_____

_____

_____

_____

_____

Is this lack of decision making getting you what you want? Is it helping or hindering you?

_____

_____

_____

_____

_____

_____

_____

Do you feel you know the difference between 'want' and 'should'? 'Should' is often derived from parental messages, cultural rules and the opinion of others, while 'want' is based more on your awareness of your tastes, talents, desires, values and interests.

_____

_____

_____

_____

_____

_____

_____

_____

Is there an overwhelming feeling that something isn't right and it's holding you back from making the necessary changes? What might that be?

_____

_____

_____

_____

_____

_____

_____

_____

How often do you listen to your inner voice and allow it to guide you towards a decision? Does it sometimes feel you get too bogged down with practical issues to allow your emotions to have their say?

_____

_____

_____

_____

_____

_____

_____

_____

Do you allow your impulses and whims to dominate the way you make decisions, spontaneously agreeing to things that aren't suitable or that you can't afford or even don't want? If so, what do you think this is about?

_____

_____

_____

_____

_____

_____

_____

_____

# Your Notes

## Your Notes

# PARENTS AND KIDS

*Knowing trees, I understand the meaning of patience.*
*Knowing grass, I can appreciate persistence.*
HAL BORLAND

Exercise, and running in particular, is an ideal way to improve the relationship you have with your children and to help them through what can often be trying stages in their young lives. Dynamic Running Therapy creates a fun and meaningful activity between you and your child, giving all of you an opportunity to discuss what is happening at home and at school. There are many benefits to running, one being that it serves as a sort of distraction, helping children to stay focused and open up about themselves. Children are also often quite excited to be running with the adults, meaning they begin from a positive and confident place. There are tips below on getting the more reluctant runners started.

Nature provides the ideal space for you to connect, as children have a natural affinity for the outdoors. It's a vibrant, spacious environment which makes sharing and bonding with your children that much easier. Unfortunately, children today are not getting enough exposure to parks, fields and forests. Richard Louv, author of *Last Child in the Woods*, introduced the term 'nature-deficit disorder' to describe the growing gap between nature and children. It is our responsibility to bridge this gap, to introduce children to the wonderment that is outside so that the wonderment that is inside them has an appropriate space in which to express itself and play.

Not only is being outdoors grounding and good for their souls, but the adventure also builds confidence. Children need to learn how to look after themselves – tracking how to get from A to B and what to do if they get lost in a forest. This builds resources they can draw on for the rest of their lives – self-reliance, curiosity and, most of all, resilience.

Most parents won't need to be told about the impact of electronics on their children and the family as a whole. They will have had front-row seats to the fighting and tears triggered by these games. As the world outside is substituted with electronic devices on the inside, it is not just the planet that loses its biodiversity, but our children too. As not just their lives, but yours too become more high-tech, it is critical that a natural balance be restored. After all, a good amount of the current anxiety epidemic is a direct consequence of lives lived out of balance.

## The Challenge Ahead

Some children, especially those who are out of shape or unsure of themselves, may struggle at first. They have the most to gain from the process. Included below are ways to make the exercises you do together more fun. In time most children will come to enjoy the open air, the green spaces and the closeness that comes from being with you.

Other children may hate exercise or find the idea of spending time with you like this 'very uncool'. For this reason, I suggest you tailor your approach to your child – start them slowly, make it fun, play one of the games-based exercises below so that it's entertaining. You may want to bring the dog, if you have one, or perhaps start with walking instead of running. Find out what works for your child.

## Tips for the Reluctant Runner

- Use a running app to measure your journey and try to outdo it by a single step or minute each time.
- Play a counting game: see who can count the most dogs, oak trees, magpies etc. List the less obvious things around you.
- See how many other runners you can greet and what kind of response you get.
- Play I-Spy.
- Alternate the green spaces you use – try a wood if the park is your usual location.

## How DRT with Your Child Works

DRT is an efficient and enjoyable way to help your child appreciate what nature has to offer. It does this through connection, natural biology and the ever-available environment. Whether on a well-trodden path in the park or cross-country running in the middle of nowhere, the time you spend running and talking together with your child is priceless and the benefits almost endless.

When you open up your adult world of running to them, children will often respond to this invitation by opening their world to you. Your child will find this special time, this experience shared by just the two of you, incredibly bonding. Couple that with the pride and sense of accomplishment that come from keeping up with you and/or attaining goals and you end up with a motivated, rejuvenated child.

Together you will experience flowing hormones such as endorphins, adrenalin and oxytocin, further bonding the two of you. Oxytocin in particular facilitates closeness, giving you an opportunity to jump start your bonding. But it is time, the greatest gift you can give your child, that will make the most difference. When they see you have dedicated this chunk of the day to them and them alone, it creates a sense of trust and closeness, and it is in that space that children find security and self-acceptance.

## Running Together

When proposing a run to your child, don't overload the description with details as this may create unnecessary pressure and be intimidating. It is often better to just say you have something fun you want to try out with them. And be warned – they might expect you to answer some questions too! Ideally, this should happen in a separate session, but the most important thing is just to get out there and get talking. Here is a suggested sequence you might want to follow:

1. If you feel it is appropriate for your child and on this day, take them through the grounding process on pages 21–5. This will help bring them into the

present moment. Some children may find it dull, but the mindfulness elements of the process may be familiar to them from school and it can be a nice opportunity to unwind together. The 'priming' question (page 24) may also encourage them to bring up troubling issues, especially as they will now be in a more relaxed state.

2. Ask your child if they feel ready to get moving.

3. Once they are ready, ask them if they prefer to walk or run.

4. Unless they have said there is something specific they want to discuss, allow the conversation to unravel naturally. After a few runs together the sessions will take on a character and life of their own. You will be surprised in what direction the conversation goes and how much honesty flows. There is no need to control the process, just allow it to happen.

5. If it feels appropriate or important, ask them a question from one of the lists below. Ask them if it is a topic they would like to discuss. You may want to agree this part in advance.

6. Listen attentively to what they are saying; that way you will know what they are really feeling.

7. Notice how their breathing and speed changes as different things are discussed. Sometimes it is useful to reflect this back to them.

8. Apply the laddering technique (page 124) if you want to know more, but be gentle and patient. Often the momentum created by running together will keep the subject going.

9. Don't expect instant results. Keep your expectations low and your sense of being present high. Enjoy.

10. Finish the session with something nice – a hug, a compliment, whatever feels right.

## Questions for You and Your Child

Who in the world do you respect and why?

What scares you in life and why?

What would you like most from your parents?

If you could do anything with your day, what would it be?

What does the word compassion mean to you? When was the last time you saw or felt it?

Do you know any perfect people?

If you had never seen nature before, what would you be like?

If you were told you would never see it again, what would you feel?

Have you ever had to forgive someone? How did it feel? How does it feel when someone's forgiven you?

What do you dream of being when you grow up? How can you achieve your dream?

When was the last time you were courageous or brave and why? How did it feel?

Do you think you can be scared and brave at the same time?

When do you feel most confident and how does it feel?

What would you say to someone who doesn't feel confident?

When did you last feel alone? How did you manage?

How does it feel when you are kind to someone and why?

When was the last time you were kind to someone you didn't know? What happened?

Sometimes we don't know what to say to someone who is sad – what other ways could you show them that you care?

Is there anything you wish you could tell someone but find it hard to?

## General Questions for Your Child

What makes you happiest?

Which is your favourite feeling and which is your worst?

If there was a way that everything could be easy, then would you choose it?

If you could be braver in one part of your life, which part would it be?

Would life be easier if you could accept your faults and everyone else's?

## Questions about School for Your Child

What did you learn in school today that you found interesting? Why?

Who don't you like at school? Why?

What are the kids at school interested in at the moment?

Who is going through a hard time at school? What are they feeling and is anyone helping them?

What does it feel like when other kids are unkind to you?

Do you feel compelled to be perfect? A perfect friend, good at sport and exams, popular and attractive? Does perfection actually exist?

Who are your closest friends? What is it that you like about them?

What do you find easy at school? What do you find
  hard?

Have you felt angry, sad or frustrated recently? How do
  you think others feel when you are angry, sad or
  frustrated? How often do you think others feel these
  emotions?

What do you think your closest friends like about you?


## Empathy Runs

An empathy run is a brief exercise specifically designed to
stimulate empathy in children. There is a programme for
schools and also one for parents with their own children.
Through a process of question, answer and summary, the
runs focus directly on increasing levels of empathy in
children.


### What is Empathy and Why is it so Important?

Roman Krznaric, cultural thinker and a founding faculty
member of The School of Life, defines empathy as 'the art
of stepping imaginatively into the shoes of another person,
understanding their feelings and perspectives, and using
that understanding to guide your actions'. We're all
empathic, right? So where's the problem? Research from
the University of Michigan shows a dramatic decline in
empathy among students over the last thirty years, with
the steepest decline reported in the last decade. Psycholo-
gists, parents and teachers are reporting an empathy crisis,
and not just in the young. No one is sure what is influenc-
ing this dramatic change – it could be overuse of technology

or gaming, superficial networks of friends, reduced partici-
pation in clubs and other social organizations, or a dozen
other possibilities. Everyone is usually too busy to sit down
and spend time with one another, and when they do the
encounter is brief and often involves electronic devices.
Children don't know any better and are learning this
behaviour from their parents.

The good news is that the researchers at the University of
Michigan believe that empathy is highly fluid, meaning
that it can potentially increase as easily as it decreases. DRT
offers exercises to help you develop your child's empathy
and your relationship with them, but make no mistake, the
most important change agent is your own behaviour. What
children want more than anything from their parents is
genuine and patient attention. Quick and superficial questions are not enough to draw them away from gaming or to
teach them the joys of good conversation. The questions
included in this chapter will help you get closer and learn
more.

## Why are Empathy Runs Important?

The camaraderie of running with you will help your children to share with you troubling topics like bullying,
dating, feeling too big or small or unattractive, not being
one of the cool kids, having a speech impediment etc.
Issues which might otherwise remain undiscussed and
become developmental problems instead get a chance to be
aired and shared. This is critical because it means your
child can understand themselves in a way that is real and
imperfect, not full of fantasy, longing and regret.

The school-based empathy runs process is carefully

designed to improve how the children relate and communicate with one another, coaching them in the practice of curiosity and 'hard listening' – listening not just to what someone is saying but to how they are saying it. Running while talking helps distract the children from whatever reservations or preconceptions they may have about the exercise, helping them to let go and enjoy it. It simultaneously adds a sense of momentum to the process, pulling the children into the topic of the day.

Below you will find many topics to explore during empathy runs. The list will help teach your child to ask questions and listen to answers – to empathize. You can do these with your children or in time they can learn to do them with each other.

## The Process

Empathy runs comprise a simple question-and-answer process conducted during a brief run. Children can be partnered by a parent, a sibling or another family member, or they work particularly well within a school peer-group environment. At school, the children can either run laps of a sports field or follow a marked route through the school grounds. They experience what it is like to step inside each other's lives – even if for only a few minutes. The process reveals to them their own abilities and interest in relating to others. As they switch roles between listener and sharer, children are often surprised by what they discover about each other, and it is through moments like these that greater empathy develops.

The school-based running programme begins with classmates being paired up and given a subject to focus on from the list below. Week 1 might be Friendships; Week 2, Happiness; Week 3, Anger and Sadness and so on. The teacher or an invited adult introduces and discusses the chosen subject, giving the exercise context and meaning.

Having discussed the topic, the partnered children embark on their run and ask the questions listed under that week's subject. They can deviate from the listed questions so long as they are consciously thinking about the topic given. After the run they rejoin the class, the listening partner giving a brief synopsis of what they heard and each partner then sharing with the other what they felt about the experience.

As children continually swap roles from speaker to listener, by term end they will all have had a chance to get to know and experience one another more deeply. A three-year study by the Canadian government into empathy training for children has shown that it results in greater 'pro-social' behaviour – like helping others and sharing – as well as improved grades, reduced bullying, improved levels of concentration in the classroom and better relationships between students and parents.

## Topics to Explore

### Learning

What is your favourite thing about school at the moment?

Do you find some of the classes hard?

How do you feel when you don't understand something?

Do you feel confident to say that you don't understand something in class?

If you didn't go to school, could you still learn things?

Do you think grown-ups still learn?

What is the best thing you have ever learned?

## Friendships

What makes a good friend?

What do you like about your friends?

Do you think you are a good friend? Why?

Do your friends ever make you feel sad?

Do you think anyone in the class feels lonely?

How could you make a friend feel better without using any words?

Do you think everyone has friends?

## Emotions

What is your favourite emotion?

What emotion do you feel most days?

What emotion would you like to feel more of?

Do your emotions ever confuse you?

Do you think grown-ups have the same emotions as children?

Do you think you can feel lots of emotions at the same time?

Do you think girls have the same emotions as boys?

## Courage

Do you ever get scared?

When was the last time you felt scared? How did it feel?

What do you do to make yourself feel better when you are scared?

Do you think grown-ups get scared?

When was the last time you were brave?

Do you think you can be scared and brave at the same time?

## Happiness

What does happiness look like?

What makes you feel happy?

Do you think you could feel happiness if sadness didn't exist?

Do you think you could be happy if you didn't have a home to live in?

Who would you like to make happy?

How would you make someone feel happier if they were sad?

What makes you feel happier when you are sad?

## Kindness

What is the kindest thing anyone has ever done for you?

What is the kindest thing you have ever done for someone?

How does it feel when you are kind?

Are you kind to people that you don't know?

Are you ever unkind?

When did you last forgive someone? Was it hard?

When you forgive someone, how does it feel afterwards?

## Patience and Compassion

What is patience?

Do you think that you are patient?

When are you impatient?

How do you feel when someone is impatient with you?

What does compassion mean to you?

Do you think it is important to have compassion? Why?

If you didn't have compassion, could you still be kind?

## Anger and Sadness

Do you ever feel angry?

When was the last time you felt angry?

When was the last time you felt sad?

When you were last angry or sad, what made you feel better? Did someone help you?

How do you think your friends feel when you are angry or sad?

What do you think about when you are sad?

Is it always the same thing that makes you sad or angry?

## Confidence

What is confidence?

Do you feel confident at school?

Where do you feel most confident?

What is it like when you don't feel confident?

Do you think that you need to feel confident all the time?

Do you think grown-ups feel confident all the time, or only sometimes?

How could you help someone feel more confident?

## Nature and the World Around Us

Do you think that children in other parts of the world feel happy?

What does a person need to be happy in the world?

What do you love about being outside?

Would you be different if you had never seen the countryside/sea? How?

If you could show someone anything outside, what would it be?

If you had one day left on the planet, what would you do?

# Your Notes

# Your Notes

# MINDFUL RUNNING

*The body benefits from movement,*
*and the mind benefits from stillness.*
SAKYONG MIPHAM RINPOCHE

As any runner knows, running is a highly rewarding activity. Its benefits include improvements in both body and mind. In addition, people who run regularly often experience greater focus and drive in their lives. Others speak of a new openness or greater spontaneity. There are many ways in which Dynamic Running Therapy can amplify that incredible energy and help you to run further and faster, getting the most out of it that you can.

For those of you who are already runners, DRT can add to the enjoyment and benefits you get from running. In this chapter the mindful running exercise variations, while similar to the others in this book, do not address any particular condition or issue. Instead they will help you get the most out of your running, improving your relationship with yourself and the green space around you.

The exercises are simple – a kind of mindful running that connects you to where and who you are. 'When mindfulness is applied to sports, it brings the mind and the body into a kind of unity,' says Jon Kabat-Zinn. The mindful running exercises in this chapter can help you to attain that state of flow which makes your running feel natural, joyful and easy. For many the struggle to improve their running is mental, an incessant inner voice telling us that we are tired, that we can't carry on and that we should probably turn round and go home. Mindful running helps quieten that voice, putting you in touch with your body and your environment. Kabat-Zinn adds: 'Running is breath by breath, footfall by footfall, moment by moment ... It has its own calming and clarifying meditative elements built right into it.' Because running and mindfulness are so similar and complementary, these exercises can quickly put you into a metronomic zone – that place where your focus and goals become one and an effortless momentum seems to sweep you along.

Mindful running builds confidence – not just in your performance but also in your sense of self and what you are capable of. While the exercises are simple the results are profound – greater mental strength and focus which you can then take into your daily life. In this way, the lessons we learn while out running can often be applied to our lives out of our trainers. Finding that energy to carry on just those few more steps, pushing through up that steep hill or enjoying the free flow of running downhill can also become metaphors for the way we approach the ups and downs of life.

Because of its emphasis on breathing, mindful running helps you to escape from the kind of negative thinking that can slow you down. 'The mind struggles less and, therefore, the body becomes more efficient,' says Sakyong Mipham Rinpoche, a leading Shambhala Buddhist monk and marathon runner. An important part of DRT is being aware of your inner thoughts and letting them pass on by, recognizing the distinction between what is a temporary thought and what is a real sensation. The reduction or limiting of negative inner dialogue is where the real performance improvement can be achieved.

A reduction in injuries is an added benefit of integrating mindful running into your exercise regime. 'You know when you can push it and when you need to back off. A lot of runners already have this knowledge, but they aren't fully aware of it and don't pay attention to it,' says George Mumford, a noted sports psychologist who teaches mindfulness techniques to professional sports teams such as the Chicago Bulls basketball team. Because your awareness of your breathing and bodily sensations is at the centre of mindful running, you are faster to notice and respond to your body's needs.

There is no suggestion that mindful running should become the only way you run. Instead consider it a way to mix things up a bit, a different approach to your running and a fresh way to come at the day. And if there are occasions when you are particularly stressed or you feel that life is pressing down on you, you may find it the ideal way to relax and let go.

Remember that, while mindful running takes practice, it is not supposed to be a burden or challenge. If you push yourself to be the best at it, to learn it quickly and perfectly, you are coming at it the wrong way. Give yourself time to find your own path – everyone's is different. You might be confronted with unexpected kinds of resistance, such as the noise in your busy head. Note the resistance, let it pass by, keep moving. You have no goal. You are not aiming for transcendence – merely letting go, emptying your mind of clutter so you can fully inhabit the present moment – *your* present moment.

## Preparing for a Mindful Run

It is best to pick a familiar route for your first few mindful runs/walks. This is so that you need not fill your mind with map-reading and anxiety about directions and distance.

To begin with you may want to just add a minute or two of mindful running to your normal run. Follow the exercises below and gradually build up your time. You may want to wait until you have got going properly before starting the mindful running – some people find it hard to go straight into mindful running, so see what style suits you. As with anything you will improve with time. Be patient. Enjoy. If you are struggling or striving, try just letting go. How hard can that be?

### Mindful-Running Exercise

Depending on your mood and how much time you have, you might want to begin your mindful run with the grounding process (see pages 21–5) – starting like this can really add to the experience. Note that you won't need to do step four of the grounding process as you are running without a focus or subject to explore.

1.  Once you are on the move, find a comfortable pace. This may be a different pace on different days, depending on your mood.

2. Take a moment or two to become mindful of the weather and your surroundings. Be conscious of the colours, smells and shapes around you.

3. Once you have a little momentum, remind yourself of your intention to run mindfully.

4. When you are ready, choose a foot, whichever feels more comfortable, and count each time it hits the ground. Remember only one foot, and the same one each time.

5. Count ten steps, beginning once more at one when you have done so. Keep this going.

6. When invasive or unhelpful thoughts come, just acknowledge they have come and then let them go, returning to your mindful running.

7. If the thoughts return, then once more let them go. It may take some time for you to get familiar with mindful running and there will be days it is harder than others.

8. If the thoughts are saying you cannot go on any longer, ask yourself if they spring from your mind or your body. If they come from your mind they are just thoughts and not the truth, let them pass on by.

9. When you find yourself in the kind of zone where the world disappears and it is just you and your steps, then you are in your flow.

10. If you want to mix things up, you can try counting your breaths instead of your steps. Be mindful of the fullness of the breath as you do so. Enjoy the sensation of filling and emptying your lungs.

## Variation 1

1. Repeat steps 1–3 above.
2. When you are ready, start to concentrate on all the sensations you are experiencing. Begin with your body – really feel the sensation of your heel as it hits the ground. Feel the breeze on your neck or as it hits the sweat on your brow. Note how the fabric of your running gear moves with each stride and how it feels against your body. Continue through the rest of your senses. This exercise is about becoming present to your body and its sensations.
3. As above, when invasive or unhelpful thoughts come, just acknowledge them and let them go before returning to your mindful running. Only sensations should be in your mind.

## Variation 2

1. Repeat steps 1–3, as before.
2. When you begin to run, look even more closely at your surroundings as you pass. Really take in the detail of what is around you. This may mean the path in front of you or the trees and flowers around you. Make this your mindful running practice. Become one with your environment. This exercise is about raising your awareness and absorbing as much of your environment as you can.
3. As above, when invasive or unhelpful thoughts come just acknowledge them and let them go before returning to your mindful running. It is only sensations that should be in your mind.

Remember, most of the limits in your running and your life are in your head. Mindful running can help you overcome these both on the path in front of you and during the rest of your life. As Kabat-Zinn says: 'The more your mind is in touch with your body, the more you can know its real limits.' So give it time – everyone has their own path and it may take a while for you to find yours, but these exercises can get you there and open up the way ahead. They can help you to meet your doubts and fears with both gentleness and wisdom. You need not slay your dragons – peace comes from letting them be. As you take to the path ahead, give them a wink as you pass them by rather than letting them pull you into a messy confrontation. Instead, enjoy the vastness of the moment you are experiencing now. That is where your strength and peace lie.

# RUNNING BACKWARDS

*If the path before you is clear,*
*you're probably on someone else's.*
JOSEPH CAMPBELL

Nobody enjoys running backwards – well, not for long, anyway. However, every journey inevitably includes setbacks. When we are metaphorically running backwards, with everyone else seemingly going in the other direction, it can feel exceptionally lonely and isolating, right at the hour of our most pressing need. And yet to strive against the unpreventable twists and turns of life is to set oneself up for disappointment upon disappointment. Reminding ourselves of life's meandering nature helps us to be more accepting and philosophical during the moments when we feel that any effort to move forward is thwarted.

Whatever we are doing, we often begin our journey with great enthusiasm, only to find there are dragons along the way. We find out we are not as well equipped for a job or a relationship as we had thought, or that others don't see us as we see ourselves. This is when the real test begins. For some these challenges take the form of a physical handicap, an abusive family environment, poverty or war. For others the battle rages inside: feelings like fear, self-loathing and depression – the stuff of daily life when doubt and fear have hold of us.

## Pride, Shame and Other Running Partners

If you find yourself running backwards during your DRT, ask yourself if there are any lessons to be learned from the experience. Pride, shame and other painful emotions can teach us much about who we are and what needs attention. We have discussed the need to acknowledge our feelings and it is no different with these. If you have met shame or pride on your journey, don't try to escape from them. Pride in particular is a wall we often build to obscure issues for which we know down deep we are at least partly accountable.

When we hide behind pride we often end up trapping the very feelings we are trying to avoid. For instance, we may think, 'I'll be damned if I admit how weak I feel in my life to you, I'm better than that,' but overcompensating thoughts like these in fact often make us weaker. They render us fractured and exhausted from the effort to maintain what isn't real. Think of the pride and shame you meet on your journey as wise men come to teach you important lessons like this, or mentors with the power to unlock a hidden treasure such as where your true strength lies.

Try to engage in this process of acceptance with as much honesty as you can muster. This is painful work – the most important lessons are often also the hardest and last ones we learn. Be truthful with yourself as you run. Have courage and faith – you will know when you meet pride and shame on the road and it is for you alone to see what lies behind them. Be patient, often it takes time to remember what it is we are hiding and where and when we hid it.

## The Mindful Struggle

Acknowledging pain and fear and seeing them for what they are – feelings and thoughts that come and go if we let them – is at the heart of mindfulness. If you have lost your way on your path and are struggling to be comfortable with a loss of momentum, inertia or sudden sense of uncertainty or fear, use the experience in a mindful way. Any of these scenarios is a good opportunity for some mindful contemplation or meditation – after all, nothing is really wrong, is it? Mostly these are just thoughts that have taken hold in your mind. They will pass if you let them. Take a breath, leave your mind, and come to the living moment.

Acknowledge the sense of being hurt or scared but don't dwell on it or fight it, or try to pretend it isn't there. Pema Chödrön, a celebrated Buddhist writer and nun, goes as far as saying we should be grateful for these moments of pain and doubt, seeing them as opportunities to grow. Try to use each moment as an opportunity to improve your practice. After all, ups and downs are out of our control, but what we do with them is not.

## Your Personal Map

In the moments you feel you are lost, you may forget everything you have learned on your journey. This is often the way. When we need it most we can't access the wisdom we have worked so hard for. For this reason, make a map with a list of directions to help you find your way in times of trouble. Spend some time finding the right name for your map. Your map is a collection of the most important things you have learned on your path – you can use the notes you have made in this book as a guide. As you go along, add to your map any skills, new mantras or directions you think you will need for your times of struggle. And when that time comes and you feel like all is lost, pull out your trusty map and take a moment to draw from your hard-won wisdom. Draw your map here, and give it a title.

**Title:**

## Acceptance

Running backwards often results from a feeling of exhaustion or being overwhelmed. After going a great distance, you finally hit what marathon runners call the 'wall' – the feeling you have hit something insurmountable. In DRT, this is most likely a part of yourself or your story you find hard to accept and make peace with. So what to do? How to find acceptance of the tougher things in life?

There is a surprisingly simple solution: acknowledgement. Acknowledgement leads to acceptance. It almost sounds too simple to be true, and yet through the straightforward practice of fully acknowledging our feelings, our experience of ourselves can change dramatically. By acknowledging fear and pain we learn to accept ourselves as we are – not as we wish we were or feel we ought to be. We can step into the world as it is, not as we would prefer it to be. This allows us more completely to occupy the living moment – not do battle with it, contorting it all in order to mask unpleasant feelings. Suddenly the weight of desire and expectation is lifted from us. As we truly allow for imperfection, counter-intuitively, in that moment, the world becomes a little more perfect.

*Note*: As many a runner will tell you, a great sense of strength, peace and contentment is to be found by going through the 'wall'. It is a sort of portal, a place where our resistance and fear gather. By acknowledging we are at the wall and then moving forward anyway, we see that we are so much more than our fears. What follows is an enormous sense of pride in our own courage and fortitude, as well as an improvement in our resilience and confidence. In these moments we often feel as though we have truly met our-selves for the first time.

## Sitting with Fear and Pain

You don't always have to experience your emotions in motion. Yet knowing when to sit down and let things be for a while can be much harder than it sounds. If there is a sense within you that you just need to stop, listen to it and see how it feels when you do. Striving to get better is like planning to be more spontaneous – it kind of works and kind of doesn't. If you have an urge to just let go for a while, or are experiencing what feels like a reversal, give yourself permission to just **let it all go**.

You might feel that by stopping you are abandoning your journey, but you could be embarking on the most important part of it. Sit down and breathe. Give yourself a chance to experience the moment. It might surprise you. Perhaps try some mindfulness exercises from the previous chapter. They will help you get out of the fear of tomorrow or the regrets of yesterday and become present. Your heart may be full of pain or your bank account almost empty, but in this very moment you are, nonetheless, alive. Remember, it is still possible to experience happiness in a far from perfect life.

## Running with Fear and Pain

If you decide to run with your fear or pain then head out with it, but don't try to fix it. If you are having a bad day, just run and see if it changes. If you like, you can explore what your expectations are around this part of your DRT journey. Make a note of them and then leave your expectations at home. Allow what needs to reveal itself or pass to have an open space in which to do so.

As ever, make a note of your running experience afterwards so you can reflect on how this part of your process works for you and in what way running helps. For some it's about being with the pain or fear and 'running it off' until it shrinks or disappears. Some of my clients report the relief they experience by not trying to avoid or fix the pain – that running during these times actually feels a bit like coming home to themselves. Others talk of surrendering to nature and a higher power. It's different for everyone. Find your own path.

## Making Peace

My clients regularly use the analogy of being at war to describe their life stories. Some talk about childhood battles for survival. Others speak of a constant need to be vigilant, to be on guard, always prepared for the next blow. I am often left in awe with a chest full of admiration and amazement for the sheer determination and courage they display. In time, once this part of their story is told, I ask them if they are still facing the same conditions, waging the same war as before. I ask if the heavy armour they wear is still needed.

It is hard to put down a trusty sword or climb off a faithful steed after a lifetime of combat. But in the promise that we will never be a victim again can lie a painful truth – we end up victimizing ourselves. We perpetuate either a war that is over or one that we no longer need to fight. Spending life battling ghosts is a tragic way to live, and yet so many of us remain committed to such an obsolete conflict.

## Letting Go

It is often said that we should pick our battles. This is sage advice indeed, but when we have only ever known war such words can feel empty. We are rightfully proud of our ability to hang on through thick and thin and loath to abandon the strength and skills that have kept us alive. I tell my clients that no one can take these from them and that I certainly have no interest in doing so. Together we acknowledge the scale and history of what they have been through and what they have suffered and managed to survive. We honour their scars and skills. And then I ask where the dragons are today.

It is often with great reluctance that we leave the front line – the trenches are often the only home we have known. We fear losing the comradeship of other soldiers whose battles are so similar and who understood what we were fighting for and the enormity of what was at stake. We worry that if we step away from the only life we have known then our endeavours will have all been for nothing.

It's so important we acknowledge how far we have come and the battles we have fought. With my clients I try to act as a witness, or a sort of historian, recording and recognizing what they have been through. And then I ask if it's possible to try a different way now. I ask, 'Do you still need to soldier on – are the bombs still dropping, are the traitors at the gate or hordes upon the wall?' It is a powerful moment when they see that the battle that rages today rages only within themselves. That in fact they are the ones keeping the dragons alive, keeping the war going.

So, as you come to this part of your journey, ask yourself if you think maybe the conditions have changed a little. Can you afford to shed some armour? Put down your weapons for a moment? Free up your hands for other things? Free up your heart for other things? Yes, the road is long and the path uncertain, but you always have a choice. Be honest and ask yourself if some of the pain and strife belongs in the past. If so, it is time you allowed yourself to take a new direction, to embark upon the next chapter in your life.

If you keep being dragged down into skirmishes with your demons, ask yourself if you can step away from this day's fighting. In this way, when you feel yourself having a bad day, falling into old habits, you can release yourself from the expectation that once more you must come out on top. Remember, walking away doesn't make you a victim, it makes you smart.

## Making Your Story Real

Owning our own story is so important. From childhood fairy tales to the novels and films that entertain us as adults, storytelling is how we understand ourselves and each other. Knowing and owning our own story, therefore, is both our responsibility and our birthright. But it can be hard – there are parts that we can't see or don't want to remember or make note of. Other parts feel unreal and confusing. In this sense our stories are mythological – as much to ourselves as to others. And often, like myths, the narrative is leading us somewhere. As the heroes of our own adventures it is up to us to choose how the tale ends. That is why the final synopsis is so important – it is your chance to truly make sense of your story so far.

When you write your synopsis (marking the end of your journey) you may or may not want to add a mythical feel to it. See if characterizing yourself as being on a hero's journey feels useful. It might feel strange, even silly, but this process can help you unlock the past and open up the path ahead. Writing, especially in this way, can help us find our courage. And on days when you feel yourself running backwards, remember that this is part of life's struggle, part of your and every other hero's journey.

# THE END OF THE RAINBOW

*You are not a drop in the ocean.*
*You are the whole ocean in a single drop.*
RUMI

There will come a point at which it begins to feel right to end your DRT process. It is important that you end it well and hold on to the gains you've made along the way. This part of the process is when you can reflect on the emotions that have surfaced during your runs and give yourself permission to put down some of your emotional baggage.

As with many of life's big decisions, such as having a baby or buying a house, there is no perfect time to start to turn a corner. There are no signs along the way saying 'Stop! Begin New Life Here'. It is equally unlikely that the fantasies you may have been holding on to will suddenly come to pass. The unconditional love you needed from your parents is probably not going to appear after all these years; neither is your perfect partner likely to show up immediately, guaranteeing you the eternal love and happiness you have always dreamed of.

Recognizing that in the final analysis you are best placed to give yourself what you need marks the moment you turn a corner for real. What you seek is within. It sits waiting to be claimed by you. Only you can provide the peace, comfort and forgiveness you long for.

*God grant me the serenity to accept the things I cannot change, the courage to change the things I can, and the wisdom to know the difference.*
REINHOLD NIEBUHR, 'SERENITY PRAYER'

Your journey has most probably included coming to an understanding that there are certain things in your life you cannot change – you can only let go of them. But really letting go of them is hard, it can feel like certain things are stuck to us like glue. Becoming unstuck involves coming to a firm conclusion as to whether it is within our power to change something or not. Often we remain in a place of fantasy – half pretending it isn't there and half hoping someone or something will cause it to shift. This serves only to perpetuate the problem as well as using up large amounts of energy. The first step is deciding if the 'something' is real rather than fantasy or possibility.

## What's in My Backpack?

Everyone has something different stuck down at the bottom of their backpack near the dirty trainers and the loose bits and pieces they carry around. And in their hearts everyone knows roughly what it is. But holding on to the real gains of Dynamic Running Therapy means more than just working out what it is in there, or learning to shoulder the weight of it. It means unpacking the bag, getting out what's in there and putting it on the ground in front of you. It means looking it right in the eye and saying, 'Good or bad, this thing exists and is mine; I'm going to stop pretending it isn't part of me.'

Looking inside yourself means really taking the time to notice how you feel about who you are. It means getting to a point where you can value yourself honestly and say, 'The truth is I don't feel good/smart/slim/strong enough.' In my work as a therapist I often find one of the most powerful moments of change comes about when my clients say out loud what they have been feeling but hiding from others all their lives. I often ask them to repeat the sentence several times so that they can own it and hear it being said. I ask them to use the simplest language possible and as few words as they can.

Ask yourself if there is an aspect of how you feel about yourself that you have never properly shared. Look inside yourself and see if there is a belief or fear you have about yourself that you have done your best to ignore, conceal or hide from others. Can it be reduced to a simple sentence? Examples I have heard in my work include: 'I am scared most of the time', 'I have never felt I was loveable', 'I have always felt like there is something bad inside me', 'I am not strong enough and must hide this from everyone'.

You may want to try saying it out loud yourself. You don't need an audience. Or perhaps you would like one. Maybe you can tell a stranger, the postman or your dog. You could try running with it or screaming it at night or on a deserted beach. For some people, to finally say it just as it is, out loud, can be hugely liberating. For others it is enough just to quietly admit it to themselves. Take your time to feel your way around this and decide what would work best for you.

It can be hard to take responsibility for the pain and shame others have instilled in us but, unfairly or not, it rests on us to make peace with it. You may not have put it there, you may have done nothing to deserve it either, but it is within you and for you to come to terms with.

Acknowledging the truth is the first step to making peace with it. Your DRT journey will bring you closer to your truth. Writing the final synopsis will help you see how it came about as well as your plan for the future. But this chapter is about making peace with it so that the gains you have made can be long-lasting.

## Different Paths

In order to make peace with the truth inside, you need to give yourself permission. And to do that, you have to feel you are worth it. Some people wake up every day for seventy years feeling they are too much this or are not enough that. They say nothing to their partner, who suffers along with them. They tell no one because they fear their truth is shameful. Others hide in the bottom of a bottle, or in overwork, or in excessive use of social media. They feel it's better to live hand on sword, prepared for a blow that may never come, rather than let down their guard and risk a serious wound to their true selves. Down this path lies the tragedy whereby one is never really known – a lonely fate indeed.

For some it is a matter of worthiness. 'How does someone like me deserve to be at peace in the world after what I have done, or as the person I have been told that I am? What do I do with all my shame, guilt and regrets?' Often this kind of self-loathing is buttressed by an enormous sadness we can't find a way of expressing, leaving us on a carousel of pain. Others can't slow down, either on the run from a traumatic past or sprinting into dreams of a better future. How can they put on the brakes and change a lifetime's momentum? How can they swim back upriver when so much water has gone under the bridge?

And then there are those so weighed down with pain, they cannot imagine ever finding a spot to put it all, unable to envision a place, person or time capable of holding the sheer quantity of unhappiness that fills their bones. So they drag it all along with them. Often these people are the unfortunate bearers of grief, sadness and other burdens that were not even theirs to carry. I think of these noble and misguided people as 'porters'. They have more to gain than anyone from checking in their luggage.

Permitting yourself to put down the pain is hard when it feels like it is the biggest part of you. It can trigger a thousand questions: What will I be without it? How will I know myself? How will I appear to others? If a smaller part is what is left, surely I shall be the weaker for it? Then how will I survive? Won't I lose everything that I have worked so hard for? If I do lose it can I regain it if needs be? The questions flow, keeping you stuck, and yet the truth is, until you begin to let go, there is no space or way to see the calm within.

Whatever the case, within each and every one of us is the possibility for forgiveness, for letting go, for starting again, for finding peace. Each of us is different. That is what makes us wonderful. We think our particular 'problem' is unforgivable or unforgettable without realizing everyone else is thinking the same thing about themselves. The story will always differ – everyone has something different to learn – but each of us is no more than a moment away from a new start.

## Reflecting on Your Journey

Throughout this book we have stressed the importance of valuing our relationship with ourselves. This is the most important thing to take onboard. You will always be imperfect; always have parts about yourself that you like less than others. The question is whether you can be gentle with them. Can you be patient? Can you listen to your needs? It is through learning to acknowledge and value our thoughts and our feelings that we go from a place of neglect to a place of care, intimacy and peace. In this way we become our own brilliant life coach, our own special confidante, our own patient listener, our own best friend.

As your write your final synopsis below or in your diary/journal (as outlined on pages 30–31), try to do so using the kind of understanding and compassionate tone with which you plan to travel forward. Remember, your path will continue to meander, your imperfections will remain, but as long as you practise self acceptance, acknowledging who and what you are, you will always be enough, just exactly as you are. Good luck and be well.

# Your Final Synopsis